The Cordial Maker's Cookbook

Make your favorite cordials, liqueurs

and aperitifs in your own kitchen

Written and Compiled by

Dennis A. Wildberger

Copyright 2014 - DocWild Publishing Company - All Rights Reserved

TABLE OF CONTENTS
Foreword

Beginning

Recipes-
Simple Syrup
Advocaat
Allspice Liqueur
Almond Liqueur
Almond Cream Cordial
Almond Shrub
Amaretto
Angelica Liqueur
Anise-Pepper Liqueur
Anisette
Apple-Cinnamon Cordial
Apricot Cordial
Banana Coconut Cream Liqueur
Banana Liqueur
Berry Gin
Blackberry Cordial
Blueberry Cordial
Cassis
Cherry Liqueur
Cherry Mint Liqueur
Cherry Rose Liqueur
Christmas Spiced Brandy
Cinnamon-Coriander Liqueur
Citrus Shrub
Citrus Vodka
Coconut-Almond Liqueur
Coconut Liqueur
Coffee Liqueur
Coffee Cream Cordial
Cossack Cough Syrup
Country Lemonade Cordial
Cran-Apple Cordial
Cranberry Cordial
Cranberry Gin
Cream Liqueur
Creme de Framboise

Creme de Menthe Liqueur
Daiquiri Liqueur
Damiana Liqueur
Damson Cordial
Date Cordial
Drambuie Liqueur
Dried Fruit Liqueur
Earl Grey Tea Liqueur
Egg Creme
Fig Cordial
Forbidden Fruits Liqueur
Fresh Mint Liqueur
Galliano Liqueur
Galingale Liqueur
Ginger Liqueur
Glog Liqueur
Grand Orange Liqueur
Hazelnut Liqueur
Honey Liqueur
Horilka
Irish Cream Liqueur #1
Irish Cream Liqueur #2
Irish Cream Liqueur #3
Irish Cream Liqueur #4
Jamaican Coffee Liqueur
Jamaican Hibiscus Liqueur
Japanese Green Tea Liqueur
Jasmine Tea Liqueur
Kiwi & Lime Liqueur
Kiwi & Strawberry Liqueur
Lemon Liqueur
Lemon Lime Liqueur
Licorice Root Liqueur
Liqueur Au Chocolat
Mango Brandy
Maple Liqueur
Marsala Cream
Mexican Coffee Cordial
Mint Cream Cordial
Mint Julep
Nectarine Liqueur
Orange & Spice Brandy
Orange Liqueur
Orange Cream Cordial
Orange Sherry

Papaya Cordial
Peach Brandy
Peach Liqueur
Peach Vanilla Cordial
Pear Cordial
Peppermint Schnapps Liqueur
Pepper Vodka
Pina Colada Cream Liqueur
Pineapple Liqueur
Plum Cordial
Plum Rum
Pomegranate Liqueur
Prune Cordial
Pumpkin Pie Liqueur
Raisin & Wine Liqueur
Raspberry Brandy
Raspberry Liqueur
Rum Cream Liqueur
Rum Shrub
Sage & Lemon Liqueur
Scottish Highland Liqueur
Sloe Gin
Spearmint Liqueur
Spiced Apple Liqueur
Spiced Rum
Spicy Orange Cordial
Spicy Pear Cordial
Star Anise Liqueur
Strawberry Liqueur
Sweet Apple Cordial
Sweet Apple Liqueur
Tangerine Liqueur
Tangerine-Nutmeg Cordial
Tart Apple Cordial
Vanilla-Coffee Liqueur
Vanilla Liqueur
Very Berry Brandy
Vin de Cerise
Walnut Liqueur
Watermelon Liqueur
Zucchini Liqueur

FOREWORD

Whether they are called liqueurs, aperitifs, cordials, or ratafias, these delicious concoctions have been around for centuries. Using only two basic ingredients, fresh fruit (or spices) and a neutral spirit, like vodka or brandy, and a simple process called "steeping" or "infusing", the sky's the limit as to what can be created.

I have been involved in the restaurant and nightclub business for more than twenty years. In that time, I have tasted commercially produced cordials and liqueurs from all over the world. Many of those that I sampled were delicious; many were not. Some were very expensive (for what you got); some were not expensive, and tasted like it. One of my favorites was (and still is) Irish Cream Liqueur. I fell in love with the flavor of this "nectar from Ireland". I enjoyed it, sometimes over-enjoyed it, every chance I could.

One day, about fifteen years ago, a co-worker, who was aware of my fondness of this beverage, gave me a recipe for "Homemade Irish Cream Liqueur". It was a simple little recipe hand-written on a white three by five card. He claimed that his mother, who was of Irish decent, made it all of the time. It seemed easy enough, so I gave it a try. It was delicious! It was easy! It was inexpensive! From that moment on, I was hooked on making cordials at home.

I began searching for recipes for other types of liqueurs that I had enjoyed in the past, but they were few and far between. So I began developing my own. By combining ingredients in an attempt to re-create some of those liqueurs I'd tasted, I came up with recipes that closely imitated the original flavors. Some, I believe, are actually better that the original. Some of the liqueurs and cordials I created are unlike any that are commercially produced.

All of the recipes in this book are tried and tested. Many appear in print for the very first time. And that recipe for Irish Cream Liqueur that got me started all those years ago, along with three other Irish Cream recipes that I have become fond of, is included here also.

Please keep in mind, these recipes are not carved in stone. By adjusting the amount of an ingredient, or the type of fruit you use, or even the aging time, you can create cordials and liqueurs that are truly personal. But do yourself a favor: write down exactly what you do and when you do it. When you invent that liqueur that is more delicious than anything you've ever tasted before; it is so much easier to make it again if you can refer to your notes.

Well, I hope that you enjoy my book, and please remember: never drink and drive.

BEGINNING

Supplies

It is always easier to gather all of the supplies you will need before you begin making cordials, rather than wasting time searching for an item as you need it.

Always wash all supplies thoroughly with soap and hot water, and dry completely before using. You can also run supplies through a dishwasher before each use. Using unclean utensils may cause mold to develop on your cordial or liqueur, rendering it useless.

Below is a list of items and their descriptions. You will not need all of these items for all of the recipes:

STEEPING AND AGING CONTAINER - A 2-quart glass or ceramic container with a tight fitting lid is always needed. If the container doesn't have a lid, try covering it with a good quality plastic wrap. Make sure it completely seals.

I have found that a half-gallon glass jar with a screw top lid works the best. Line the inside of the lid with a layer of plastic wrap or waxed paper while using.

Never use a metal container to steep or age you cordials. Metal may cause a chemical reaction to occur within your recipe, changing its color or flavor, producing some really nasty stuff.

BLENDER OF FOOD PROCESSOR - Use these items only if the recipe calls for it. Most of the time, a better cordial is produced if the fruit or spices are chopped by hand. It is also easier to strain and filter your cordials if there is a bit of size to the fruit.

SHARP KNIFE AND CUTTING BOARD - For cutting the fruit and spices to usable size.

SLOTTED METAL OR WOODEN SPOON - Used for mashing fruit before using, and stirring your cordial per recipe directions.

FINE MESH SIEVE - Used for straining your cordial prior to aging.

CHEESECLOTH - Available at most grocery and notion stores, this tightly woven linen cloth is used for straining your cordials. It is excellent for separating the solids from the liquids. If cheesecloth is not available, you can use a funnel lined with dampened coffee filters with similar results. The filters do tend to clog a lot quicker, so you will need to change them several times during straining.

MORTAR AND PESTLE - Used for crushing fresh spices. A small clean coffee grinder also works very well if mortar and pestle are not available.

MEASURING CUPS AND MEASURING SPOONS - Helps you accurately measure the ingredients in you recipe. Remember that it is easier to duplicate a recipe later if you know exactly how much you put in it now.

SELECTING FRUITS AND SPICES

When selecting fruit for a specific recipe, choose only the freshest available. Under-ripe fruit will not produce a quality product. Allow fruit to ripen to its peak before using. It is all right to use over-ripe fruit, but discard any fruit that has even the slightest evidence of molding or severe bruising. Many grocers will discount the price of over-ripe fruit or fruit that is slightly blemished. These fruits are excellent for cordial recipes, provided they are not moldy.

Choose recipes with fruits that are in season. It makes better economical sense to make, say, Peach Brandy, in the summertime when peaches are in season and less expensive.

Same is true of spices. Use only fresh spices when available. Fresh ground spices, such as nutmeg and ginger, are far more superior in flavor than commercially ground bottled spices. Bottled spices lose their essence and taste with time. If bottled spices are all that is available, you can still use them. However, you may need to increase the amount in specific recipes to achieve the same result as fresh.

AGING AND STORING

During the steeping and aging process, always store your cordial in a cool, dark place. A kitchen cabinet where the temperature is a constant 50 to 70 degrees is perfect. Avoid areas over ovens or next to refrigerators. The temperature fluctuations from these appliances may have an adverse effect on your cordial.

Always keep your cordials tightly capped. If left open, any number of bad things could happen to your product. Fruit flies, mold, dust, and evaporation are all enemies of cordials, and will cause your cordial to deteriorate faster.

BOTTLING

It is always a great thrill to share the cordials you've made with family and friends. I like to purchase decorative bottles or decanters, fill with my newest cordial, and give them as gifts for holidays or birthdays.

Many department stores have a small selection of bottles. Many "dollar" stores also carry a nice inexpensive selection. I have also found some beautiful bottles in thrift stores and at yard sales.

Regardless of where you find your bottles or decanters, always wash them thoroughly before filling. A run through the dishwasher, or a bath in boiling water will kill any germs or remove any dust.

Provided the bottles are sealed tightly, some cordials and liqueurs will continue to age after being bottled, but don't count on that. As a general rule, always allow your cordials to age according to the method and length of time described in the recipe prior to bottling. If you do this, you can always be assured that when that bottle is opened, an excellent cordial will be enjoyed.

RECIPES

SIMPLE SYRUP

Simple syrup is the basis of most of the recipes in this book. As a real time-saver, it is best to make the syrup in advance, and keep tightly sealed in the refrigerator.

Makes about 4 cups

4 cups sugar
2 cups water

Combine sugar and water in heavy medium saucepan, stirring to mix; heat over medium heat to boiling. Reduce heat; simmer until sugar has completely dissolved, about 3 minutes. Remove from heat; cool syrup to room temperature before using. Store, covered, in refrigerator; syrup will keep indefinitely.

TIP: Microwave directions: Place 4 cups sugar and 2 cups water in microwave-safe bowl; stir to mix. Microwave, covered with microwave-safe plastic wrap, on high power until mixture is boiling, about 3 minutes. Remove from oven; stir until sugar dissolves and solution is clear. Cool to room temperature before using.

ADVOCAAT

For a delicious treat, try drizzling a bit of this cordial over a scoop of vanilla ice cream.

Makes about 4 cups

1 1/4 cups sugar
3/4 teaspoon vanilla extract
1/2 teaspoon lemon extract
1 cup vodka
5 eggs
1 egg yolk
2/3 cup evaporated milk

Combine all ingredients in a blender; process on high for 1 minute. Pour liqueur into a 2-quart glass or ceramic container; cap tightly, or cover tightly with plastic wrap. Let liqueur age in the refrigerator for 2 weeks, swirling mixture around in container occasionally. Store in refrigerator up to 1 month.

TIP: 1 1/4 cups of brandy may be substituted for the vodka; brandy will produce a slightly mellower flavor.

ALLSPICE LIQUEUR

This is a fragrant and pungent liqueur that
is excellent for those cold winter evenings.

Makes about 4 cups

1 1/2 teaspoons ground Allspice
3 cups vodka
1 cup Simple Syrup

Combine ground allspice and vodka in a 2-quart glass or ceramic container; stir to mix. Cap tightly, or cover tightly with plastic wrap. Let liqueur steep in a cool dark place for 2 weeks, swirling mixture around in container every 3 days.

Strain liqueur through sieve lined with double thickness of dampened cheesecloth into clean container. Thoroughly wash and dry original container, or have ready a second clean glass or ceramic container. Set funnel or coffee cone lined with dampened filter paper or coffee filter over container; slowly pour liqueur through.

Add Simple Syrup to liqueur; stir to mix. Cap tightly; let age for 4 weeks, swirling mixture around in container once a week. Re-filter liqueur. Store in an airtight container.

TIP: Brandy may be substituted for the Vodka for a mellower cordial.

ALMOND LIQUEUR

Almond liqueur is often produced commercially under the name of "Creme de Noya" or "Creme de Noyeaux".

Makes about 6 cups

3 cups sugar
2 1/4 cups water
Rinds of 3 lemons, finely grated
4 cups vodka
3 tablespoons almond extract
3 tablespoons vanilla extract

Combine the sugar, water, and grated lemon rinds in a medium saucepan; heat over a medium flame, stirring consistently as not to scorch; bring to a slow boil. Reduce heat and let mixture simmer for 5 minutes, stirring occasionally; remove from heat. Let cool to room temperature. When cooled, stir in vodka, almond extract, and vanilla extract.

Transfer the liqueur to a glass or ceramic container; cap tightly or cover tightly with plastic wrap. Let age in a cool dark place for about 3 weeks, swirling mixture around in container every 3 to 4 days.

If a sediment develops after 3 weeks, discontinue the swirling and allow sediment to settle to the bottom of the container (about 1 week). Set funnel or coffee cone containing dampened filter paper or coffee filter over a second clean glass or ceramic container; slowly pour liqueur through. When liqueur is filtered to desired clarity, test for sweetness; add simple syrup to taste. Cap tightly.

TIP #1: Flavor is the best if liqueur is used within 4 months.
TIP #2: When this liqueur is completely filtered, a couple of drops of red food coloring may be stirred in.

ALMOND CREAM CORDIAL

Here is a quick an easy recipe using a portion of the
Almond Liqueur from the previous recipe.

Makes about 5 cups

1 14-ounce can sweetened condensed milk
1 1/4 cup almond liqueur
1 cup whipping cream
4 eggs

Combine sweetened condensed milk, almond liqueur, whipping cream, and eggs in a blender. Process at medium speed for approximately 1 minute. Transfer cordial to an air- tight glass or ceramic container; cap tightly. Let cordial age in the refrigerator overnight before using.

TIP: This cordial can be stored for up to 1 month. Refrigerate any unused portion.

ALMOND SHRUB

Shrub is another name for cordial. Shrubs are popular beverages in parts of England.

Makes about 6 cups

**4 cups light rum
1 cup fresh orange juice
Rind of 1 lemon, sliced, pith removed
4 cups sugar
1 cup whole milk
10 drops of almond extract**

   Combine rum, orange juice, lemon peel, and sugar in a 2-quart glass or ceramic container. Stir until the sugar has dissolved. In a mixing glass, combine the milk and almond extract; stir, and let sit until it reaches room temperature. Pour the milk mixture into the juice mixture. Cap tightly, or cover tightly with plastic wrap. Set in a warm place (65 to 70 degrees Fahrenheit) until the milk has curdled, usually around 3 hours. Set funnel or coffee cone containing dampened filter paper or coffee filter over a second clean glass or ceramic container; slowly pour liqueur through. Let liqueur age for 2 weeks, swirling mixture around in container occasionally.

   Refrigerate after aging, and serve cold. This liqueur is best when consumed within 3 weeks of completing the aging process.

AMARETTO

This is a quick and easy recipe that comes pretty close to reproducing the classic Italian favorite. For an even richer flavor, try using 4 dried apricot halves, and 1/4 cup fresh sliced almonds.

Makes about 4 cups

1 cup Simple Syrup
2 dried apricot halves
1 tablespoon almond extract
3/4 cup vodka
1/2 cup water
1 cup brandy
3 drops yellow food coloring
6 drops red food coloring
2 drops blue food coloring
1/2 teaspoon glycerin

Combine simple syrup, dried apricot halves, almond extract, vodka, water, and brandy in a 2-quart glass or ceramic container; stir to mix. Cap tightly, or cover tightly with plastic wrap. Let cordial steep in a cool dark place for 1 week, swirling mixture around in container daily.

Remove apricot halves; stir in yellow, red, and blue food coloring, and glycerin. Re-cover container. Let cordial age 4 more weeks.

TIP: This cordial will continue to age for up to 1 year, but is best enjoyed before that time.

ANGELICA LIQUEUR

This unusual liqueur has been produced for centuries in Europe.

Makes about 4 cups

**3 tablespoons dried Angelica root, chopped
1 tablespoon chopped almonds
1 allspice berry, cracked
1 1-inch cinnamon stick
6 anise seeds, crushed
1/8 teaspoon powdered coriander
1 tablespoon fresh marjoram leaves, minced
2 1/2 cups vodka
1 1/2 cup Simple Syrup
1 drop yellow food coloring
1 drop green food coloring**

Combine angelica root, chopped almonds, allspice berry, cinnamon stick, crushed anise seeds, powdered coriander, marjoram leaves, and vodka in a 2-quart glass or ceramic container; cap tightly, or cover tightly with plastic wrap. Let liqueur steep in a cool dark place for 2 weeks, swirling mixture around in container each day.

Strain liqueur through sieve lined with double thickness of dampened cheesecloth into clean container. Thoroughly wash and dry original container, or have ready a second clean glass or ceramic container. Set funnel or coffee cone lined with dampened filter paper or coffee filter over container; slowly pour liqueur through. Add simple syrup and food colorings; stir. Cover tightly; let age 4 weeks in a cool dark place.

ANISE-PEPPER LIQUEUR

Here is a most unusual recipe that combines two distinctive flavors into one heart-warming liqueur.

Makes about 4 cups

4 cups vodka
1 cup sugar
6 whole star anise
8 whole black peppercorns, crushed

Combine vodka, sugar, anise, and crushed peppercorns in a glass or ceramic container; stir until the sugar is completely dissolved. Cap tightly or cover tightly with plastic wrap. Let age in a cool dark place for about 2 weeks, swirling mixture around in container every 3 to 4 days.

Set funnel or coffee cone containing dampened filter paper or coffee filter over a second clean glass or ceramic container; slowly pour liqueur through. When liqueur is filtered to desired clarity, test for sweetness; add simple syrup to taste. Cap tightly.

ANISETTE

Here is another recipe that closely reproduces a classic Italian cordial. Anisette has long been used as an after-dinner aperitif to aid in digestion.

Makes about 4 cups

3 tablespoons star anise seeds, crushed
2 cups vodka
2 cups Simple Syrup
1 tablespoon glycerin

Combine crushed anise seeds, vodka and simple syrup in a 2-quart glass or ceramic container; cap tightly, or cover tightly with plastic wrap. Let liqueur steep in a cool dark place for 4 weeks, swirling mixture around in container each day.

Strain liqueur through sieve lined with double thickness of dampened cheesecloth into clean container. Thoroughly wash and dry original container, or have ready a second clean glass or ceramic container. Set funnel or coffee cone lined with dampened filter paper or coffee filter over container; slowly pour liqueur through. When liqueur is filtered to desired clarity, test for sweetness. Add additional simple syrup to taste; add glycerin; stir. Cover tightly; let age 4 more weeks in a cool dark place.

APPLE-CINNAMON CORDIAL

This cordial is delicious and sweet, and will
remind you of homemade apple pie.

Makes about 4 cups

4 cups vodka
3 cups sugar
3 whole cinnamon sticks, broken
4 large Red Delicious apples, cored & sliced

Combine vodka, sugar, broken cinnamon sticks, and sliced apples in a glass or ceramic container; stir until the sugar is completely dissolved. Cap tightly or cover tightly with plastic wrap. Let age in a cool dark place for about 3 weeks, swirling mixture around in container every 3 to 4 days.

When a sediment develops after about 2 weeks, discontinue the swirling and allow sediment to settle to the bottom of the container (about 1 week). Set funnel or coffee cone containing dampened filter paper or coffee filter over a second clean glass or ceramic container; slowly pour liqueur through. When liqueur is filtered to desired clarity, test for sweetness; add simple syrup to taste. Cap tightly.

TIP #1: Flavor is the best if liqueur is used within 4 months.

APRICOT CORDIAL

I have tried making this recipe using fresh apricots, but the quality and flavor is much richer using the dried fruit.

Makes about 4 cups

3/4 pound dried apricots
2 cups Simple Syrup
2 cups vodka

Slice apricots in half. Combine apricot halves, simple syrup, and vodka in a 2-quart glass or ceramic container; stir to mix. Cap tightly, or cover tightly with plastic wrap. Let liqueur age in a cool dark place for 4 weeks, swirling mixture around in container every 3 days.

Strain cordial through sieve lined with double thickness of dampened cheesecloth into clean container. Thoroughly wash and dry original container, or have ready a second clean glass or ceramic container. Set funnel or coffee cone lined with dampened filter paper or coffee filter over container; slowly pour cordial through. When cordial is filtered to desired clarity, test for sweetness. Adjust sweetness by adding additional simple syrup. Cover tightly; let age 4 to 8 weeks in a cool dark place.

BANANA COCONUT CREAM LIQUEUR

This tropical concoction will make you wish you were on an island beach in the Caribbean.

Makes about 4 cups

**2 very ripe bananas
2 teaspoons coconut extract
1 1/2 cups rum
1/2 cup vodka
1/2 cup sweetened condensed milk
1/2 cup evaporated milk
1 cup cream of coconut**

Mash bananas, and combine in a blender with the coconut extract, rum, and vodka. Process on high, then reduce blender speed to low after ingredients are well blended. Slowly pour in the sweetened condensed milk and the evaporated milk. Continue processing on low speed. Add cream of coconut.

Transfer mixture to a 2-quart glass or ceramic container; cap tightly, or cover tightly with plastic wrap. Refrigerate, and let sit for about 1 week, swirling occasionally. Serve cold.

TIP: This cordial is best if used within 1 month.

BANANA LIQUEUR

This is an excellent recipe. The flavor of the finished product far exceeds any banana liqueur that is commercially available.

Makes about 4 1/2 cups

1 cup Simple Syrup
3 1/2 cups mashed ripe banana
(about 6 large bananas)
2 cups light rum
2 cups vodka
1 tablespoon plus 2 teaspoons *Fruit Fresh* *
2 teaspoons vanilla extract

Combine mashed banana, rum, vodka, 1 tablespoon *Fruit Fresh*, and vanilla extract in 2-quart glass or ceramic container. Cap tightly or cover tightly with plastic wrap. Let steep in a cool dark place 2 weeks, swirling mixture around in container every 3 days.

Strain mixture through a sieve lined with double thickness of dampened cheesecloth into clean container; discard contents of sieve. Thoroughly wash and dry original container, or have ready a second clean glass or ceramic container. Set funnel or coffee cone containing dampened filter paper or coffee filter over container; slowly pour liqueur through. When liqueur is filtered, test for sweetness. Add simple syrup to taste and 1 to 2 teaspoons *Fruit Fresh as* necessary to preserve color. Cover tightly; let liqueur age 4 to 6 weeks in a cool dark place. This liqueur may take a long time to clear. If you decide not to filter it until it is entirely clear, don't worry; a slight cloudiness will not affect the taste.

TIP: * Fruit Fresh is available in most supermarkets where canning supplies are sold.

BERRY GIN

This flavored gin is a nice variation
of the standard Sloe Gin.

Makes about 4 cups

***2 pound assorted berries, slightly mashed
3 cups sugar
4 cups gin**

  Combine mashed berries, sugar, and gin in a glass or ceramic container; stir until the sugar is completely dissolved. Cap tightly or cover tightly with plastic wrap. Let age in a cool dark place for about 4 weeks, swirling mixture around in container every other day.

  Set funnel or coffee cone containing dampened filter paper or coffee filter over a second clean glass or ceramic container; slowly pour liqueur through. When liqueur is filtered to desired clarity, test for sweetness; add simple syrup to taste. Cap tightly.

*TIP: Good berries for this recipe includes raspberries, strawberries, and blueberries. Use a good even mix when combining berries.

BLACKBERRY CORDIAL

Here is a delicious cordial to make when
you have an abundance of sweet blackberries.

Makes about 4 cups

4 cups blackberries
3 cups bottled water
4 whole cloves
3 black peppercorns
3 cardamon pods, lightly crushed
2 cinnamon sticks, broken into pieces
1 large bay leaf
1 cup light brown sugar
1 1/2 cups Cognac or brandy

In a medium saucepan, combine the blackberries, bottled water, cloves, peppercorns, cardamon, cinnamon pieces, and bay leaf. Bring just to a boil, reduce heat, and simmer on low flame for 30 minutes, stirring constantly, gently crushing the blackberries against the side of the pan. Remove from heat.

Strain through sieve lined with double thickness of dampened cheesecloth into a glass or ceramic container, taking care not to press on the berries. Add brown sugar, and stir until dissolved. Let cool completely.

Stir in the Cognac or brandy. Cover tightly; let age 4 weeks in a cool dark place. Depending on the clarity of this cordial after the aging process, you may need to strain and filter it again.

BLUEBERRY CORDIAL

Here is a great opportunity to turn a bountiful summer
harvest of blueberries into a cordial that can
be enjoyed on a cool autumn evening.

Makes about 4 cups

4 cups blueberries
3 cups vodka
1/4 fresh lemon juice
1/2 teaspoon coriander seeds
4 whole cloves
3 cups Simple Syrup

Wash and drain blueberries; crush berries with the back of a large spoon. Combine crushed blueberries, vodka, lemon juice, coriander seeds, cloves, and simple syrup in a 2-quart glass or ceramic container; stir to mix. Cap tightly, or cover tightly with plastic wrap. Let cordial steep in a cool dark place for 2 weeks, swirling mixture around in container every other day.

Strain cordial through sieve lined with double thickness of dampened cheesecloth into clean container. Thoroughly wash and dry original container, or have ready a second clean glass or ceramic container. Set funnel or coffee cone lined with dampened filter paper or coffee filter over container; slowly pour cordial through. When cordial is filtered to desired clarity, test for sweetness; add additional simple syrup to taste. Cover tightly; let age 4 weeks in a cool dark place.

CASSIS

If currants are not available, dark raisins may be substituted with similar success.

Makes about 4 cups

**2 pounds black currants
2 cups brandy
2 cups sugar
Simple Syrup**

Coarsely chop currants in a food processor or a blender. Combine currants, brandy, and sugar in a 2-quart glass or ceramic container; cap tightly, or cover tightly with plastic wrap. Let cordial steep in a cool dark place for 6 weeks, swirling mixture around in container once a week.

Strain cordial through sieve lined with double thickness of dampened cheesecloth into clean container. Thoroughly wash and dry original container, or have ready a second clean glass or ceramic container. Set funnel or coffee cone lined with dampened filter paper or coffee filter over container; slowly pour cordial through. When cordial is filtered to desired clarity, test for sweetness. Adjust sweetness by adding simple syrup. Cover tightly; let age 4 weeks in a cool dark place.

TIP: If liqueur is not clear after final aging, you may want to re-filter. Follow the same process as before.

CHERRY LIQUEUR

This is a wonderful liqueur to enjoy as an aperitif with family and friends before a nice dinner.

Makes about 4 cups

5 cups sweet Bing cherries, pitted
1 1/2 cups simple syrup
3 cups vodka
5 drops lemon extract

In a 2-quart glass or ceramic container, lightly chop the cherries. Add simple syrup, vodka, and lemon extract. Stir to mix. Cap tightly, or cover tightly with plastic wrap. Let liqueur age in a cool dark place for 4 weeks, swirling mixture around in container every 3 days.

Strain cordial through sieve lined with double thickness of dampened cheesecloth into clean container. When cordial is filtered to desired clarity, test for sweetness. Adjust sweetness by adding additional simple syrup. Cover tightly; let age 2 to 4 weeks in a cool dark place.

TIP: After straining the liqueur, don't throw away the cherries. They make a great topping for ice cream or pound cake.

CHERRY MINT LIQUEUR

This is a delicious variation of the previous recipe.

Makes about 4 cups

**5 cups sweet cherries, pitted
20 crushed cherrystones
20 fresh mint leaves
thinly sliced peel of 1 lemon
4 cups vodka
1 cup sugar**

Coarsely chop the cherries, reserving as much juice as possible. Combine chopped cherries and juice, crushed cherrystones, mint leaves, and sliced lemon peel in 2-quart glass or ceramic container. Add sugar and vodka. Stir until all of the sugar is dissolved. Cap tightly or cover tightly with plastic wrap. Let steep in a sunny window for at least 2 weeks, swirling mixture around in container every day.

Strain mixture through a sieve lined with double thickness of dampened cheesecloth into clean container; discard contents of sieve. Thoroughly wash and dry original container, or have ready a second clean glass or ceramic container. Set funnel or coffee cone containing dampened filter paper or coffee filter over container; slowly pour liqueur through. When liqueur is filtered, test for sweetness. Add simple syrup to taste. Cover tightly; let liqueur age 4 to 6 weeks in a cool dark place.

TIP: Cherry stones can easily be crushed using a mortar and pedstal, or by placing them in a small plastic bag and hitting repeatedly with a hammer.

CHERRY ROSE LIQUEUR

Here is another interesting variation of the
Cherry Liqueur recipe on the previous page.

Makes about 5 cups

5 cups sweet cherries, pitted and chopped
3/4 cup cherry preserves
1/4 cup rose syrup
2 cups simple syrup
4 cups vodka

Combine chopped cherries, cherry preserves, rose syrup, simple syrup, and vodka in a glass or ceramic container; stir to mix. Cap tightly or cover tightly with plastic wrap. Let age in a cool dark place for about 4 weeks, swirling mixture around in container every other day.

Set funnel or coffee cone containing dampened filter paper or coffee filter over a second clean glass or ceramic container; slowly pour liqueur through. When liqueur is filtered to desired clarity, test for sweetness; add simple syrup to taste. Cap tightly; let liqueur age for an additional 4 to 6 weeks.

TIP: Rose syrup may be found at a good East Indian grocer.

CHRISTMAS SPICED BRANDY

This is a delicious cordial that is wonderful when served at the holidays, or to give as gifts.

Makes about 4 cups

1 cinnamon stick, broken
4 whole allspice, crushed
3 whole cloves, crushed
1/4 teaspoon grated fresh gingerroot
1/4 teaspoon grated nutmeg
Peel of 1 tangerine, thinly sliced
1 1/2 cups brown sugar
4 cups brandy

Combine broken cinnamon stick, crushed allspice, crushed cloves, grated ginger root, grated nutmeg, sliced tangerine peel, brown sugar, and brandy in a glass or ceramic container; stir until all of the sugar is dissolved. Cap tightly or cover tightly with plastic wrap. Let age in a cool dark place for about 4 weeks, swirling mixture around in container every 3 or 4 days.

Set funnel or coffee cone containing dampened filter paper or coffee filter over a second clean glass or ceramic container; slowly pour liqueur through. When liqueur is filtered to desired clarity, test for sweetness; add simple syrup to taste. Cap tightly; let liqueur age for an additional 3 to 4 weeks.

TIP: If liqueur is not clear after final aging, you may want to re-filter. Follow the same process as before.

TIP #2: I have tried making this recipe with store-bought ground spices, but it was very difficult to get a clear liqueur. The taste was not as good either.

CINNAMON-CORIANDER LIQUEUR

This is a deliciously spicy liqueur that is fabulous served on a cold winter afternoon.

Makes about 4 cups

1 1/2 cups vodka
1 1/2 cups brandy
4 whole cinnamon sticks, broken
3 teaspoons ground coriander
4 whole cloves, lightly crushed
10 raisins
1 cup simple syrup

Combine vodka, brandy, broken cinnamon sticks, ground coriander, crushed cloves, raisins, and simple syrup in a glass or ceramic container; stir to combine all ingredients. Cap tightly or cover tightly with plastic wrap. Let age in a cool dark place for about 4 weeks, swirling mixture around in container every 3 or 4 days.

Set funnel or coffee cone containing dampened filter paper or coffee filter over a second clean glass or ceramic container; slowly pour liqueur through. When liqueur is filtered to desired clarity, test for sweetness; add simple syrup to taste. Cap tightly; let liqueur age for an additional 3 to 4 weeks.

TIP: If liqueur is not clear after final aging, you may want to re-filter. Follow the same process as before.

CITRUS SHRUB

Here is another English-style shrub.
This one is delightfully refreshing
served ice cold.

Makes about 6 cups

**4 cups light rum
1 cup fresh orange juice
1 cup fresh lemon juice
Rind of 1 lemon, sliced, pith removed
4 cups sugar**

Combine rum, orange juice, lemon juice, lemon peel and sugar in a 2-quart glass or ceramic container. Stir until the sugar has dissolved. Cap tightly, or cover tightly with plastic wrap. Let cordial steep in a cool dark place for 2 weeks, swirling mixture around in container every 3 days.

Remove peels. Strain cordial through sieve lined with double thickness of dampened cheesecloth into clean container. Thoroughly wash and dry original container, or have ready a second clean glass or ceramic container. Set funnel or coffee cone lined with dampened filter paper or coffee filter over container; slowly pour cordial through. When cordial is filtered to desired clarity, test for sweetness; add simple syrup to taste.   Cover tightly and let cordial age for an additional 2 to 4 weeks.

CITRUS VODKA

Served ice cold, this liqueur is excellent with a wedge of fresh lemon dipped in granulated sugar.

Makes about 6 cups

5 cups vodka
4 large lemons, or 6 large limes
1/2 cup Simple Syrup

Peel lemons or limes, removing inner white pith from rind; reserve pulp for other use. Cut peels into 2 inch by 1/4-inch strips. Combine fruit peels and vodka in a 2-quart glass or ceramic container; add simple syrup; stir to mix. Cap tightly, or cover tightly with plastic wrap. Let liqueur steep in a cool dark place for 3 weeks, swirling mixture around in container every 3 days.

Remove peels. Strain liqueur through sieve lined with double thickness of dampened cheesecloth into clean container. Thoroughly wash and dry original container, or have ready a second clean glass or ceramic container. Set funnel or coffee cone lined with dampened filter paper or coffee filter over container; slowly pour liqueur through. Store in an airtight container.

COCONUT-ALMOND LIQUEUR

This liqueur is delicious served over crushed ice.

Makes 1 1/2 to 2 cups

1 cup Simple Syrup
2 medium fresh coconuts
1 1/4 cups vodka
1 1/4 cups light rum
3 ounces sliced almonds
1 vanilla bean, split
1 3-inch cinnamon stick

Heat oven to 350 F

Pierce coconut eyes with an ice pick or nail. Drain off coconut juice; discard or save for another use. Bake coconuts on oven rack until shells are cracked, about 15 minutes. Tap shells with a hammer to open; remove coconut meat. Pare brown skin from coconut meat; cut meat into 1-inch pieces. Process pieces of coconut, in batches, in food processor or blender. Measure 3 cups of grated coconut, packing tightly; reserve remainder for other use.

Combine coconut, vodka, rum, almonds, vanilla bean, and cinnamon stick in a 2-quart glass or ceramic container. Cap tightly or cover tightly with plastic wrap. Let steep 2 weeks in a cool dark place, swirling mixture around in container every 3 days.

Drain coconut in medium-mesh sieve set over 4-cup measure, pressing with the back of a large spoon to extract as much liquid as possible; discard contents of sieve. Strain liquid through clean sieve lined with double thickness of dampened cheesecloth into clean container. Thoroughly wash and dry original container, or have ready a second clean glass or ceramic container. Set funnel or coffee cone containing dampened filter paper or coffee filter over container; slowly pour liqueur through. When liqueur is filtered to desired clarity, test for sweetness; add simple syrup to taste. Cap tightly; let age about 1 month in a cool dark place.

COCONUT LIQUEUR

Commercially processed coconut does not work as well as fresh coconut. However, if processed is all that is available, increase to 4 cups of shredded coconut mixed with 2 tablespoons of coconut extract.

Makes about 2 cups

1 cup Simple Syrup
2 medium fresh coconuts
2 cups vodka
3 whole coriander seeds

Heat oven to 350 F.

Pierce coconut eyes with an ice pick or nail. Drain off coconut juice; discard or save for another use. Bake cocnuts on oven rack until shells are cracked, about 15 minutes. Tap shells with a hammer to open; remove coconut meat. Pare brown skin from coconut meat; cut meat into 1-inch pieces. Process pieces of coconut, in batches, in food processor or blender. Measure 3 cups of grated coconut, packing tightly; reserve remainder for other use.

Combine coconut, vodka, and coriander seeds in a 2-quart glass or ceramic container. Cap tightly or cover tightly with plastic wrap. Let steep 3 weeks in a cool dark place, swirling mixture around in container every 3 days.

Drain coconut in medium-mesh sieve set over 4-cup measure, pressing with the back of a large spoon to extract as much liquid as possible; discard contents of sieve. Strain liquid through clean sieve lined with double thickness of dampened cheesecloth into clean container. Thoroughly wash and dry original container, or have ready a second clean glass or ceramic container. Set funnel or coffee cone containing dampened filter paper or coffee filter over container; slowly pour liqueur through. When liqueur if filtered to desired clarity, test for sweetness; add simple syrup to taste. Cap tightly; let age about 1 month in a cool dark place.

COFFEE LIQUEUR

This international favorite can be made at any time of the year using ingredients readily available in your kitchen.

Makes about 5 cups

3 1/2 cups sugar
2 cups water
2 ounces instant coffee
1 vanilla bean, split
2 cups bourbon

Combine water, sugar, and instant coffee in a medium saucepan. Heat over a medium flame until boiling, stirring constantly so as not to let the mixture scorch. Continue to boil until all sugar is dissolved; remove from heat; let cool to room temperature.

Pour coffee mixture into a 2-quart glass or ceramic container; add bourbon and vanilla bean; stir. Cap container tightly, or cover tightly with plastic wrap; store in a cool dark place. Let liqueur age 6 to 8 weeks, swirling mixture in container every week or so.

TIP #1: This liqueur has the best flavor if it is aged 6 months or longer; however, it may be consumed after 2 months.
TIP #2: 2 tablespoons of vanilla extract may be substituted for the vanilla bean.

COFFEE CREAM CORDIAL

Using the coffee liqueur from the previous recipe,
try making this delicious cordial.

Makes about 5 cups

1 14-ounce can sweetened condensed milk
1 1/4 cup coffee liqueur
1 cup whipping cream
4 eggs

Combine sweetened condensed milk, coffee liqueur, whipping cream, and eggs in a blender. Process at medium speed for approximately 1 minute. Transfer cordial to an air- tight glass or ceramic container; cap tightly. Let cordial age in the refrigerator overnight before using.

TIP: This cordial can be stored for up to 1 month. Refrigerate any unused portion.

COSSACK COUGH SYRUP

This liqueur is thick and rich, and
not exactly to everyone's taste.

Makes about 5 cups

**5 cups vodka
1/2 pound dried black currants
1/2 pound dried apricots, chopped
1 1/2 cups dried hibiscus flowers
1 cup hyssop
2 limes, thinly sliced
1 lemon, thinly sliced
1/4 cup star anise
1 teaspoon dried whole fennel seed
2 cups sugar
1 cup dried lemon balm
20 dried juniper berries**

Combine vodka, currants, chopped apricots, hibiscus flowers, hyssop, sliced limes, sliced lemon, star anise, and fennel seeds in a 2 quart glass or ceramic container; stir well. Add sugar; stir until all of the sugar has dissolved. Cap tightly, or cover tightly with plastic wrap. Let cordial steep in a cool dark place for 2 weeks, swirling mixture around in container every other day.

Strain cordial through sieve lined with double thickness of dampened cheesecloth into clean container, reserving the raw items. Place the strained raw materials in a 4-quart non-stick pot. Add 2 cups of water, the dried lemon balm, and the juniper berries. Simmer on a low heat until you can smell the juniper berries, about 20 minutes. Remove from heat and let cool.

Strain newly cooked liqueur through sieve lined with double thickness of dampened cheesecloth into clean container. Combine alcoholic liqueur together with the second liqueur; stir. Test for sweetness. At this point, you can adjust the liqueur to suit your taste. You may add additional sugar, stirring until sugar is completely dissolved, or add additional vodka.

Thoroughly wash and dry original container, or have ready a second clean glass or ceramic container. Set funnel or coffee cone lined with dampened filter paper or coffee filter over container; slowly pour cordial through. Cover tightly and let cordial age for an additional 4 to 8 weeks.

TIP: Many of the ingredients necessary in this recipe may be found at a good health food grocer, or an herbal shop.

COUNTRY LEMONADE CORDIAL

Serve this cordial over ice with a slice of fresh lemon.

Makes about 5 cups

4 large lemons
2 cups Simple Syrup
2 cups bourbon
1/4 cup fresh lemon juice

Peel lemons , removing inner white pith from rind; reserve pulp. Cut peels into 2 inch by 1/4-inch strips. Combine lemon peels, lemon juice, and bourbon in a 2-quart glass or ceramic container; add simple syrup; stir to mix. Cap tightly, or cover tightly with plastic wrap. Let cordial steep in a cool dark place for 4 weeks, swirling mixture around in container every 3 days.

Remove peels. Strain cordial through sieve lined with double thickness of dampened cheesecloth into clean container. Thoroughly wash and dry original container, or have ready a second clean glass or ceramic container. Set funnel or coffee cone lined with dampened filter paper or coffee filter over container; slowly pour cordial through. When cordial is filtered to desired clarity, test for sweetness; add simple syrup to taste. Cover tightly and let cordial age for an additional 4 to 8 weeks.

CRAN-APPLE CORDIAL

This delicious cordial will remind you of the
holiday season any time of the year.

Makes about 3 cups

1 cup Simple Syrup
2 cups coarsely chopped fresh cranberries
2 tart green apples, such as Granny Smith,
pared, cored, coarsely chopped (about
2 cups)
1 cup brandy
1 cup vodka
1 teaspoon vanilla extract
6 whole cloves
1 cinnamon stick

Combine cranberries, apples, 1 cup simple syrup, the brandy, vodka, vanilla extract, cloves, and cinnamon stick in a 2-quart glass or ceramic container. Cap tightly or cover tightly with plastic wrap. Let steep 3 weeks in cool dark place, swirling mixture around in container every 3 days.

Drain fruit in a coarse sieve set over 4-cup glass measure, pressing gently but firmly with the back of a large spoon to extract as much liquid as possible.

Strain cordial through a clean sieve lined with double thickness of dampened cheesecloth into a clean container. Thoroughly wash and dry original container, or have ready a second container. Set funnel or coffee cone containing dampened filter paper or coffee filter over container; slowly pour cordial through. When cordial is filtered to desired clarity, test for sweetness. Adjust sweetness to taste with additional simple syrup, if desired. Cover tightly; let cordial age 3 to 4 weeks in a cool dark place.

CRANBERRY CORDIAL

Cranberry lovers will not find a better
cordial produced commercially.

Makes about 4 cups

**1- 12 ounce package fresh cranberries
1 cup sugar
2 cups light corn syrup
2 cups vodka
1 cup water 1/2
cup brandy**

Coarsely chop the cranberries in a food processor fitted with a metal blade, or roughly chop with a sharp knife. Pour the chopped cranberries into a 2-quart glass or ceramic container; add sugar. Stir the cranberries until they are well coated. Mix in the corn syrup, vodka, water, and brandy, stirring to blend. Cap the container tightly, or cover tightly with plastic wrap. Let mixture steep for at least 4 weeks, swirling or shaking container every 3 days.

Drain cranberry mixture in medium-mesh sieve set over 4-cup measure, pressing with the back of a large spoon to extract as much liquid as possible; discard contents of sieve. Strain liquid through clean sieve lined with double thickness of dampened cheesecloth into clean container. Thoroughly wash and dry original container, or have ready a second clean glass or ceramic container. Set funnel or coffee cone containing dampened filter paper or coffee filter over container; slowly pour liqueur through. When liqueur if filtered to desired clarity, test for sweetness; add simple syrup to taste. Cap tightly; let age about 1 month in a cool dark place.

CRANBERRY GIN

Here is an interesting variation of
the previous recipe.

Makes about 4 cups

2- 12 ounce package fresh cranberries
4 cups sugar
3 cups gin

  Coarsely chop the cranberries in a food processor fitted with a metal blade, or roughly chop with a sharp knife. Pour the chopped cranberries into a 2-quart glass or ceramic container; add sugar. Stir the cranberries until they are well coated. Mix in the gin, stirring to blend. Cap the container tightly, or cover tightly with plastic wrap. Let mixture steep for at least 4 weeks, swirling or shaking container every 3 days.

  Drain cranberry mixture in medium-mesh sieve set over 4-cup measure, pressing with the back of a large spoon to extract as much liquid as possible; discard contents of sieve. Strain liquid through clean sieve lined with double thickness of dampened cheesecloth into clean container. Thoroughly wash and dry original container, or have ready a second clean glass or ceramic container. Set funnel or coffee cone containing dampened filter paper or coffee filter over container; slowly pour liqueur through. When liqueur if filtered to desired clarity, test for sweetness; add simple syrup to taste. Cap tightly; let age about 1 month in a cool dark place.

CREAM LIQUEUR

This easy recipe is wonderful when served iced cold.

Makes about 4 cups

3 eggs
1 15-ounce can sweetened condensed milk
1 cup dark rum
1 cup heavy cream
4 teaspoons instant coffee
1/4 teaspoon coconut extract
1/2 teaspoon ground cinnamon
1/2 teaspoon vanilla extract
1/4 cup chocolate syrup

  Combine all ingredients in a clean blender; process on high for approximately 1 minute. Transfer liqueur to a large glass or ceramic container; cap tightly or cover tightly with plastic wrap. For best flavor, allow liqueur to stand in the refrigerator overnight or up to 2 weeks before serving.

TIP: To prevent spoilage, keep liqueur refrigerated.

CREME de FRAMBOISE

This is a wonderfully delightful cordial,
and is one of my all-time favorites.

Makes about 4 cups

2 cups ripe black raspberries
3 cups brandy
1/2 cup dry white wine
1 tablespoon fresh lemon zest
1 cup simple syrup

Lightly crush the raspberries. Combine crushed raspberries, fresh lemon zest, brandy, and white wine in a 2-quart glass or ceramic container; stir. Cap container tightly, or cover tightly with plastic wrap; store in a cool dark place. Let liqueur age 2 to 4 weeks, swirling mixture in container every week or so.

Strain cordial through sieve lined with double thickness of dampened cheesecloth into clean container. Thoroughly wash and dry original container, or have ready a second clean glass or ceramic container. Set funnel or coffee cone lined with dampened filter paper or coffee filter over container; slowly pour cordial through. When cordial is filtered to desired clarity, add simple syrup. Cover tightly and let cordial age for an additional 4 to 8 weeks.

TIP: This liqueur has the best flavor if it is aged 6 months or longer; however, it may be consumed after 2 months.

CREME de MENTHE LIQUEUR

The green (with food coloring) or clear (without food coloring) version of this liqueur is excellent served over crushed ice, or mixed with a little fresh half-and-half.

Makes about 6 cups

2 cups fresh peppermint leaves
4 cups vodka
2 cups Simple Syrup
1/2 teaspoon peppermint oil
2 to 3 drops green food coloring (optional)

Rinse peppermint leaves under cold running water. Carefully mince leaves with a sharp knife. Combine minced peppermint leaves and vodka in a 2-quart glass or ceramic container; stir to mix. Cap tightly, or cover tightly with plastic wrap. Let liqueur steep in a cool dark place for 2 weeks, swirling mixture around in container every 3 days.

Strain liqueur through sieve lined with double thickness of dampened cheesecloth into clean container. Thoroughly wash and dry original container, or have ready a second clean glass or ceramic container. Set funnel or coffee cone lined with dampened filter paper or coffee filter over container; slowly pour liqueur through. When liqueur is filtered to desired clarity, add simple syrup, peppermint oil, and green food coloring. Cover tightly; let age 2 to 4 weeks in a cool dark place.

TIP: If liqueur is not clear after final aging, you may want to re-filter. Follow the same process as before.

DAIQUIRI LIQUEUR

Try this liqueur processed in a blender
with a cup of crushed ice.

Makes about 4 cups

**4 large fresh limes
3 cups light rum
1 1/2 cups sugar**

Peel limes, removing inner white pith from rind; reserve lime pulp for other use. Cut peels into 2 inch by 1/4-inch strips; blot peels with a paper towel to remove excess oil. Combine lime peels and 2 cups of the rum in a 2-quart glass or ceramic container; cap tightly, or cover tightly with plastic wrap. Let liqueur steep in a cool dark place for 1 week, swirling mixture around in container every other day.

Strain liqueur through sieve lined with double thickness of dampened cheesecloth into clean container. Thoroughly wash and dry original container, or have ready a second clean glass or ceramic container. Set funnel or coffee cone lined with dampened filter paper or coffee filter over container; slowly pour liqueur through. Add sugar and 1 cup of rum; stir until all sugar is dissolved. Cover tightly; let age 4 weeks in a cool dark place.

DAMIANA LIQUEUR

It has been reported that this liqueur has "aphrodisiac" qualities.

Makes about 5 cups

**1 1/2 ounce dried Damiana leaves
3 cups pure grain alcohol
4 cups water
1 cup honey**

Combine the dried Damiana leaves, the grain alcohol, and 2 cups of water in a 2-quart glass or ceramic container. Cap tightly or cover tightly with plastic wrap. Let steep 2 weeks in cool dark place, swirling mixture around in container every 3 days.

After 2 weeks, strain off the Damiana leaves. In a separate container (a 2 quart glass jar with a tight fitting cap works well), add the strained Damiana leaves and 2 cups of water. Shake well.

Let both containers sit in a cool, dark place for an additional 2 weeks or longer.

After two weeks or so, strain off the Damiana leaves from the second container. Discard leaves. In a medium saucepan, combine the water from the second container and 1 cup of honey. Stir constantly over a low heat until the honey is dissolved. Remove from heat and let cool. Combine both the alcohol mixture and the water/honey mixture; cap tightly. Let liqueur age undisturbed for 1 month.

Strain liquid through clean sieve lined with double thickness of dampened cheesecloth into clean container. When liqueur if filtered to desired clarity, test for sweetness; add simple syrup to taste.

DAMSON CORDIAL

This is a delicious cordial that makes
excellent use of this summer fruit.

Makes about 5 cups

2 lbs. sliced & pitted ripe damsons
2 cups simple syrup
3 cups vodka

Combine sliced damsons, simple syrup, and vodka in a 2-quart glass or ceramic container; stir to mix. Cap tightly, or cover tightly with plastic wrap. Let cordial steep in a cool dark place for 4 weeks, swirling mixture around in container every 3 days.

Strain cordial through sieve lined with double thickness of dampened cheesecloth into clean container. Thoroughly wash and dry original container, or have ready a second clean glass or ceramic container. Set funnel or coffee cone lined with dampened filter paper or coffee filter over container; slowly pour cordial through. When cordial is filtered to desired clarity, test for sweetness; add simple syrup to taste. Cover tightly and let cordial age for an additional 2 to 4 weeks. This is one of those cordials that certainly does improve with age.

DATE CORDIAL

This cordial has an unusual color,
but it certainly is tasty.

Makes about 4 cups

**1 cup simple syrup
1 lb. coarsely chopped pitted dates
3 cups vodka**

Combine chopped dates, simple syrup, and vodka in a 2-quart glass or ceramic container. Cap tightly or cover tightly with plastic wrap. Let steep 3 weeks in cool dark place, swirling mixture around in container every other day.

Drain fruit in a coarse sieve set over 4-cup glass measure, pressing gently but firmly with the back of a large spoon to extract as much liquid as possible.

Strain cordial through a clean sieve lined with double thickness of dampened cheesecloth into a clean container. Thoroughly wash and dry original container, or have ready a second container. Set funnel or coffee cone containing dampened filter paper or coffee filter over container; slowly pour cordial through. When cordial is filtered to desired clarity, test for sweetness. Adjust sweetness to taste with additional simple syrup, if desired. Cover tightly; let cordial age 3 to 4 weeks in a cool dark place.

DRAMBUIE LIQUEUR

Drambuie is a Scottish liqueur with a very distinctive flavor. This easy recipe is very close to the original product.

Makes about 4 cups

**2 cups Simple Syrup 1　
teaspoon anise extract　
2 cups Scotch　
1 tablespoon glycerin***

Combine simple syrup, anise extract, Scotch, and glycerin in a 2-quart glass or ceramic container; stir to mix. Cap tightly, or cover tightly with plastic wrap. Let liqueur steep in a cool dark place for 3 weeks, swirling mixture around in container every 3 days.

TIP: * Glycerin is available at most drug stores or pharmacies.

DRIED FRUIT LIQUEUR

As this recipe is written, it is very good.
You may experiment with assorted dried fruits
for a completely different liqueur.

Makes about 4 cups

1 cup dried peaches, chopped
1/2 cup dried cherries
6 dried black figs, sliced
1 cup simple syrup
3 cups dry white wine
1/2 cup brandy

Combine sliced dried peaches, dried cherries, sliced figs, simple syrup, white wine, and brandy in a 2-quart glass or ceramic container; stir to mix. Cap tightly, or cover tightly with plastic wrap. Let liqueur steep in a cool dark place for 4 weeks, swirling mixture around in container every 3 days.

Drain fruit mixture in medium-mesh sieve set over a clean glass bowl, pressing with the back of a large spoon to extract as much liquid as possible; discard contents of sieve. Strain liquid through clean sieve lined with double thickness of dampened cheesecloth into clean container. Thoroughly wash and dry original container, or have ready a second clean glass or ceramic container. Set funnel or coffee cone containing dampened filter paper or coffee filter over container; slowly pour liqueur through. When liqueur is filtered to desired clarity, test for sweetness; add simple syrup to taste. Cap tightly; let age about 1 month in a cool dark place.

EARL GREY TEA LIQUEUR

Here is an interesting, easy to make liqueur that
surely will become one of your favorites.

Makes about 4 cups

6 Earl Grey teabags
3 cups vodka
1 cup simple syrup
1 teaspoon glycerin

Combine tea bags and vodka in a 2-quart glass or ceramic container. Cap tightly, or cover tightly with plastic wrap. Let steep for no more than 24 hours; if the tea bags steep for any longer, the liqueur may take on a bitter flavor. Remove tea bags and discard.

Add simple syrup and glycerin to the vodka/tea mixture; stir and cap tightly. Let age about 2 months in a cool dark place. This liqueur is best when consumed within one month after aging process.

TIP: You may opt to use a good quality loose tea for this recipe. If you do, then only steep the tea in the vodka for 15 to 18 hours. You will then have to filter the liqueur using dampened coffee filters prior to adding the simple syrup and the glycerin.

EGG CREME

This liqueur is delicious poured over crushed ice,
or drizzled over a scoop of vanilla ice cream.

Makes about 4 cups

8 egg yolks
1 cup sugar
1/4 teaspoon vanilla extract
1 can (15 ounces) sweetened
condensed milk
2 1/2 cups brandy
1/2 cup water 1
cinnamon stick

Beat egg yolks in large mixer bowl until light; beat in sugar and vanilla extract until mixture is pale and creamy, about 2 minutes. Beat in condensed milk until well blended; stir in brandy and water until thoroughly combined. Pour mixture through fine-mesh strainer into a clean container; repeat one or more times until no sediment remains. Pour liqueur into a 2-quart glass or ceramic container; add cinnamon stick. Cap tightly or cover tightly with plastic wrap. Let age in a cool dark place for at least 3 months and up to 1 year;* shake container weekly for the first month, or until there is no separation.

Remove cinnamon stick; pour aged liqueur into a clean decanter of desired size. Cap tightly. Liqueur will keep up to 5 months after opening or longer if refrigerated.

TIP: Although the liqueur will be mellow enough for consumption after the 3-month minimum, the maximum aging time is recommended for really superb flavor.

FIG CORDIAL

Using dried black figs will produce a cordial with a much richer color.

Makes about 4 cups

12 ounces dried figs
2 cups Simple Syrup
1 1/2 cups brandy

  Combine dried figs, simple syrup, and brandy in a 2-quart glass or ceramic container; cap tightly, or cover tightly with plastic wrap. Let cordial steep in a cool dark place for 4 weeks, swirling mixture around in container every 3 days.

  Strain cordial through sieve lined with double thickness of dampened cheesecloth into clean container. Thoroughly wash and dry original container, or have ready a second clean glass or ceramic container. Set funnel or coffee cone lined with dampened filter paper or coffee filter over container; slowly pour cordial through. When cordial is filtered to desired clarity, test for sweetness. Adjust sweetness by adding additional simple syrup Store in an airtight container. Cover tightly; let age 4 weeks in a cool dark place.

FORBIDDEN FRUITS LIQUEUR

This wonderful and fresh recipe is delicious when served ice cold.

Makes about 4 cups

Peel of 1 orange, thinly sliced
Peel of 1 lemon, thinly sliced
1 cup fresh grapefruit juice
1 cup fresh orange juice
1/4 cup fresh lemon juice
2 cups sugar
4 vanilla beans, split
1 cup brandy
1 cup vodka

   In a medium saucepan, combine orange peel, lemon peel, grapefruit juice, orange juice, lemon juice, sugar, and split vanilla beans. Heat over a very low flame, stirring constantly. Bring to a slow simmer until all of the sugar has been dissolved. Remove from heat. Let cool.

   Transfer mixture to a large glass or ceramic container. Add brandy and vodka; stir to mix. Cap tightly or cover tightly with plastic wrap. Age in a cool, dark place for 3 weeks.

   Strain liqueur through sieve lined with double thickness of dampened cheesecloth into clean container. Thoroughly wash and dry original container, or have ready a second clean glass or ceramic container. Set funnel or coffee cone lined with dampened filter paper or coffee filter over container; slowly pour liqueur through. When liqueur is filtered to desired clarity, add more simple syrup to taste. Liqueur is ready to drink now, but for better flavor, let age 2 to 4 additional weeks in a cool dark place.

FRESH MINT LIQUEUR

The green (with food coloring) or clear (without food coloring) version of this liqueur is excellent served over crushed ice, or mixed with a little fresh half-and-half.

Makes about 4 cups

2 cups fresh spearmint leaves
3 cups vodka
1 cup simple syrup
1 teaspoon glycerin
2 to 3 drops green food coloring (optional)

Rinse spearmint leaves under cold running water. Carefully mince leaves with a sharp knife. Combine minced spearmint leaves and vodka in a 2-quart glass or ceramic container; stir to mix. Cap tightly, or cover tightly with plastic wrap. Let liqueur steep in a cool dark place for 2 weeks, swirling mixture around in container every 3 days.

Strain liqueur through sieve lined with double thickness of dampened cheesecloth into clean container. Thoroughly wash and dry original container, or have ready a second clean glass or ceramic container. Set funnel or coffee cone lined with dampened filter paper or coffee filter over container; slowly pour liqueur through. When liqueur is filtered to desired clarity, add simple syrup, glycerin, and green food coloring (if desired). Cover tightly; let age 2 to 4 weeks in a cool dark place.

TIP: If liqueur is not clear after final aging, you may want to re-filter. Follow the same process as before.

GALLIANO LIQUEUR

This delicious Italian favorite is excellent served over ice, or shaken with fresh orange juice.

Makes about 6 cups

2 cups Simple Syrup
1/4 cup anise extract
1 teaspoon vanilla extract
4 cups vodka
3 drops yellow food coloring (optional)
1 tablespoon glycerin*

Combine simple syrup, anise extract, vanilla extract, vodka, yellow food coloring, and glycerin in a 2-quart glass or ceramic container;   stir to mix. Cap tightly, or cover tightly with plastic wrap. Let liqueur age in a cool dark place for 3 weeks, swirling mixture around in container every 3 days.

TIP:* Glycerin is available at most drug stores or pharmacies.

GALINGALE LIQUEUR

Galingale is an exotic form of ginger,
available in some international food shops.

Makes about 4 cups

2 teaspoons dried galingale
1 teaspoon fresh ginger, grated
1 cinnamon stick, broken
2 whole cloves
10 raisins
3 cups vodka
1 cup simple syrup
1 teaspoon glycerin

Combine dried galingale, freshly grated ginger, cinnamon stick, cloves, raisins, and vodka in a 2-quart glass or ceramic container. Cap tightly, or cover tightly with plastic wrap. Let liqueur steep in a cool dark place for 1 week, swirling mixture around in container every day.

Strain liqueur through sieve lined with double thickness of dampened cheesecloth into clean container. Thoroughly wash and dry original container, or have ready a second clean glass or ceramic container. Set funnel or coffee cone lined with dampened filter paper or coffee filter over container; slowly pour liqueur through. Add simple syrup and glycerin; stir well. Cover tightly; let age 4 additional weeks in a cool dark place.

TIP: This is a spicy liqueur, but if you like it even spicier, double the amount of galingale that you use.

GINGER LIQUEUR

This is a simpler variation of the previous recipe, but not quite as spicy.

Makes about 4 cups

2 teaspoons fresh ginger, grated
1 cinnamon stick, broken
2 whole cloves
10 raisins
3 cups vodka
1 cup simple syrup
1 teaspoon glycerin

    Combine freshly grated ginger, cinnamon stick, cloves, raisins, and vodka in a 2-quart glass or ceramic container. Cap tightly, or cover tightly with plastic wrap. Let liqueur steep in a cool dark place for 2 weeks, swirling mixture around in container every day.

    Strain liqueur through sieve lined with double thickness of dampened cheesecloth into clean container. Thoroughly wash and dry original container, or have ready a second clean glass or ceramic container. Set funnel or coffee cone lined with dampened filter paper or coffee filter over container; slowly pour liqueur through. Add simple syrup and glycerin; stir well. Cover tightly; let age 4 additional weeks in a cool dark place.

GLOG LIQUEUR

In it's truest form, Glog is not a cordial or liqueur. It is a traditional Swedish holiday drink. I developed this liqueur as a variation of the original recipe.

Makes about 6 cups

2 cups red port wine
2 cups vodka
4 cardamon pods
10 whole cloves
1 orange peel, thinly sliced
1 cinnamon stick, broken
12 raisins
2 fresh almonds, thinly sliced
2 cups simple syrup

In a medium saucepan, combine red port wine, vodka, cardamon pods, cloves, sliced orange peel, cinnamon stick, raisins, and almonds. Heat over a very low flame, stirring constantly. Bring to a slow simmer, then remove from heat. Let cool.

Transfer mixture to a large glass or ceramic container. Add simple syrup; stir to mix. Cap tightly or cover tightly with plastic wrap. Age in a cool, dark place for 2 weeks.

Strain liqueur through sieve lined with double thickness of dampened cheesecloth into clean container. Thoroughly wash and dry original container, or have ready a second clean glass or ceramic container. Set funnel or coffee cone lined with dampened filter paper or coffee filter over container; slowly pour liqueur through. When liqueur is filtered to desired clarity, add more simple syrup to taste.

GRAND ORANGE LIQUEUR

Some commercial versions of this liqueur have been aged in wooden casks for 100 years or longer.

Makes about 4 cups

1/2 cup fresh orange zest
1 1/2 cup Simple Syrup
2 cups cognac
1/2 teaspoon glycerin

   Combine orange zest and cognac in a 2-quart glass or ceramic container; add simple syrup; stir to mix. Cap tightly, or cover tightly with plastic wrap. Let liqueur steep in a cool dark place for 8 weeks, swirling mixture around in container once a week.

   Strain liqueur through sieve lined with double thickness of dampened cheesecloth into clean container. Thoroughly wash and dry original container, or have ready a second clean glass or ceramic container. Set funnel or coffee cone lined with dampened filter paper or coffee filter over container; slowly pour liqueur through. When liqueur is filtered to desired clarity, test for sweetness; add additional simple syrup to taste. Add glycerin; stir to mix. Cover tightly; let age 2 additional months, or up to 1 year, in a cool dark place.

TIP: The best oranges to use for this recipe are bitter Haitian oranges or Sevilles.

HAZELNUT LIQUEUR

To get the best flavor, use only freshly shelled hazelnuts.

Makes about 4 cups

1/2 pound hazelnuts, finely chopped
3 cups vodka
1 cup Simple Syrup
2 teaspoons vanilla extract

In a 2-quart glass or ceramic container, combine chopped hazelnuts and vodka; cap tightly or cover tightly with plastic wrap. Let mixture steep in a cool dark place for at least 3 weeks, swirling contents around in container every other day.

Strain liqueur through sieve lined with double thickness of dampened cheesecloth into clean container. Thoroughly wash and dry original container, or have ready a second clean glass or ceramic container. Set funnel or coffee cone lined with dampened filter paper or coffee filter over container; slowly pour liqueur through. Add simple syrup and vanilla extract; stir. Re-cover container and allow liqueur to age at least 3 more weeks.

HONEY LIQUEUR

Each time you make this recipe, try using a different kind of honey. The subtle differences in honey flavors and colors will produce unique liqueurs.

Makes about 4 cups

2 cups pure honey
1/2 cup hot water
2 cups brandy

Combine honey and hot water in a 2-quart glass or ceramic container; stir until honey is dissolved; add brandy. Cap tightly, or cover tightly with plastic wrap. Let liqueur age in a cool dark place for 4 weeks, swirling mixture around in container once a week

HORILKA

This is an ancient recipe that dates from early 1600's.

Makes about 5 cups

2 cups water
2 cinnamon sticks, broken
1 whole nutmeg, cracked
8 whole cloves
3 cardamon pods
1 teaspoon ground allspice
1/2 teaspoon fennel
Peel of 1 lemon, thinly sliced
Juice of 1 lemon
2 cups honey
1 cup apple juice
3 cups brandy

In a medium saucepan, combine water, cracked nutmeg, cloves, cardamon pods, ground allspice, fennel, lemon peel, lemon juice, and honey. Heat over a very low flame, stirring constantly. Bring to a slow simmer, then remove from heat. Let cool.

Transfer mixture to a large glass or ceramic container. Add apple juice and brandy; stir to mix. Cap tightly or cover tightly with plastic wrap. Age in a cool, dark place for 4 weeks. Shake gently each day for the first 2 weeks, then allow to rest for the following 2 weeks.

Slowly strain liqueur through sieve lined with double thickness of dampened cheesecloth into clean container. Thoroughly wash and dry original container, or have ready a second clean glass or ceramic container. Set funnel or coffee cone lined with dampened filter paper or coffee filter over container; slowly pour liqueur through. When liqueur is filtered to desired clarity, add more simple syrup to taste. Age in a cool, dark place for 4 additional weeks.

Each of these four recipes for Irish Cream Liqueur produce a similar product, but are all distinctly different. Try making each one, and decide for yourself which recipe you prefer.

IRISH CREAM LIQUEUR #1

Makes about 4 cups

3 eggs
1 15-ounce can sweetened condensed milk
1 cup whipping cream
1/2 teaspoon coconut extract
3 tablespoons chocolate syrup
3 cups Scotch Whiskey

Combine all ingredients in a clean blender; process on high for approximately 1 minute. Transfer liqueur to a large glass or ceramic container; cap tightly or cover tightly with plastic wrap. For best flavor, allow liqueur to stand in the refrigerator overnight or up to 2 weeks before serving.

TIP: To prevent spoilage, keep liqueur refrigerated.

IRISH CREAM LIQUEUR #2

Makes about 4 cups

2 cups half and half
1 cup sweetened condensed milk
2 cups 80 proof whiskey
1 teaspoon instant coffee
2 ounces coffee liqueur

Combine all ingredients in a clean blender; process on high for approximately 1 minute. Transfer liqueur to a large glass or ceramic container; cap tightly or cover tightly with plastic wrap. For best flavor, allow liqueur to stand in the refrigerator overnight or up to 2 weeks before serving.

TIP: To prevent spoilage, keep liqueur refrigerated.

IRISH CREAM LIQUEUR #3

Makes about 5 cups

2 eggs
1 15-oz. can sweetened condensed milk
2 tablespoons chocolate syrup
1 tablespoon vanilla extract
1 1/2 tablespoons instant coffee
1/3 cup boiling water
1 cup whipping cream
1 1/3 cups Irish whiskey

Dissolve instant coffee in boiling water; let cool to room temperature.

Combine all ingredients in a clean blender; process on high for approximately 1 minute. Transfer liqueur to a large glass or ceramic container; cap tightly or cover tightly with plastic wrap. For best flavor, allow liqueur to stand in the refrigerator overnight or up to 2 weeks before serving.

TIP: To prevent spoilage, keep liqueur refrigerated

IRISH CREAM LIQUEUR #4

Makes about 4 cups

2 eggs
2 cups sweetened condensed milk
1 cup 80 proof whiskey
1 1/2 cups Non-Dairy Creamer
3 tablespoons chocolate syrup

Combine all ingredients in a clean blender; process on high for approximately 1 minute. Transfer liqueur to a large glass or ceramic container; cap tightly or cover tightly with plastic wrap. For best flavor, allow liqueur to stand in the refrigerator overnight or up to 2 weeks before serving.

TIP: To prevent spoilage, keep liqueur refrigerated

JAMAICAN COFFEE LIQUEUR

The commercial version of this liqueur has been produced since the time when pirates sailed the Caribbean.

Makes about 4 cups

2 cups hot water
2 cups dark brown sugar
4 tablespoons instant coffee
2 cups dark rum
4 tablespoons vanilla extract

Combine hot water, brown sugar, and instant coffee in a medium saucepan. Heat over a low flame until mixture comes to a slow simmer, stirring constantly to avoid scorching. Simmer for 2 minutes; remove from heat; allow to cool to room temperature. Transfer coffee/sugar mixture to a 2-quart glass or ceramic container; add rum and vanilla extract; stir to mix. Cap tightly, or cover tightly with plastic wrap. Let liqueur steep in a cool dark place for 4 weeks, swirling mixture around in container once a week.

Strain liqueur through sieve lined with double thickness of dampened cheesecloth into clean container. Thoroughly wash and dry original container, or have ready a second clean glass or ceramic container. Set funnel or coffee cone lined with dampened filter paper or coffee filter over container; slowly pour liqueur through. When liqueur is filtered to desired clarity, test for sweetness; add additional simple syrup to taste. Cover tightly; let age 2 weeks in a cool dark place.

JAMAICAN HIBISCUS LIQUEUR

Once you have enjoyed this fragrant liqueur,
you will want to make it over and over again.

Makes about 6 cups

**4 cups water
1 cup dried hibiscus blossoms*
1/2 teaspoon fresh ginger, grated
1/2 cup sugar
2 cups Jamaican rum**

In a medium saucepan, bring water to boil; add the hibiscus blossoms, grated ginger, and sugar; turn off heat and cover with a tight-fitting lid. Let mixture cool to room temperature. Pour mixture into a 2-quart glass or ceramic container; add rum. Cap tightly, or cover tightly with plastic wrap. Let liqueur steep for 4 weeks in a cool dark place, swirling mixture around in container once a week.

Strain liqueur through sieve lined with double thickness of dampened cheesecloth into clean container. Thoroughly wash and dry original container, or have ready a second clean glass or ceramic container. Set funnel or coffee cone lined with dampened filter paper or coffee filter over container; slowly pour liqueur through. Store in an airtight container. This liqueur is best if served cold.

TIP: Dried hibiscus blossoms can usually be found in Jamaican or Mexican markets. They are sometimes known as "sorrel blossoms".

JAPANESE GREEN TEA LIQUEUR

Here is an interesting, easy to make liqueur with a light, fresh aftertaste.

Makes about 4 cups

6 teaspoons loose green tea
3 cups vodka
1 cup simple syrup
1 teaspoon glycerin
3 drops green food coloring

Combine tea and vodka in a 2-quart glass or ceramic container. Cap tightly, or cover tightly with plastic wrap. Let steep for no more than 24 hours.

Strain liqueur through sieve lined with double thickness of dampened cheesecloth into clean container. Thoroughly wash and dry original container, or have ready a second clean glass or ceramic container. Set funnel or coffee cone lined with dampened filter paper or coffee filter over container; slowly pour liqueur through.

Add simple syrup, food coloring, and glycerin to the vodka/tea mixture; stir and cap tightly. Let age about 2 months in a cool dark place. This liqueur is best when consumed within one month after aging process.

JASMINE TEA LIQUEUR

This is another interesting tea liqueur that
is delicious when served after dinner.

Makes about 4 cups

6 teaspoons loose jasmine tea
3 cups dark rum
1 cup simple syrup 1
teaspoon glycerin

   Combine tea and dark rum in a 2-quart glass or ceramic container. Cap tightly, or cover tightly with plastic wrap. Let steep for no more than 24 hours.

   Strain liqueur through sieve lined with double thickness of dampened cheesecloth into clean container. Thoroughly wash and dry original container, or have ready a second clean glass or ceramic container. Set funnel or coffee cone lined with dampened filter paper or coffee filter over container; slowly pour liqueur through.

   Add simple syrup and glycerin to the rum/tea mixture; stir and cap tightly. Let age about 2 months in a cool dark place. This liqueur is best when consumed within one month after aging process.

KIWI & LIME LIQUEUR

I love this liqueur served ice
cold direct from the freezer.

Makes about 4 cups

10 kiwis, sliced
1 cup fresh lime juice
Peel of 1 lime, thinly sliced
3 cups vodka
1 cup simple syrup

Combine sliced kiwis, lime juice, lime peel, simple syrup, and vodka in a 2-quart glass or ceramic container; stir to mix. Cap tightly, or cover tightly with plastic wrap. Let liqueur steep in a cool dark place for 4 weeks, swirling mixture around in container every 3 days.

Drain fruit mixture in medium-mesh sieve set over a clean glass bowl, pressing with the back of a large spoon to extract as much liquid as possible; discard contents of sieve. Strain liquid through clean sieve lined with double thickness of dampened cheesecloth into clean container. Thoroughly wash and dry original container, or have ready a second clean glass or ceramic container. Set funnel or coffee cone containing dampened filter paper or coffee filter over container; slowly pour liqueur through. When liqueur is filtered to desired clarity, test for sweetness; add simple syrup to taste. Cap tightly; let age about 1 month in a cool dark place.

KIWI & STRAWBERRY LIQUEUR

Here is another kiwi liqueur that is delicious served ice cold direct from the freezer.

Makes about 4 cups

10 kiwis, sliced
2 cups fresh strawberries, sliced
Peel of 1 lemon, thinly sliced
3 cups vodka
1 cup simple syrup

Combine sliced kiwis, sliced strawberries, lemon peel, simple syrup, and vodka in a 2-quart glass or ceramic container; stir to mix. Cap tightly, or cover tightly with plastic wrap. Let liqueur steep in a cool dark place for 4 weeks, swirling mixture around in container every 3 days.

Drain fruit mixture in medium-mesh sieve set over a clean glass bowl, pressing with the back of a large spoon to extract as much liquid as possible; discard contents of sieve. Strain liquid through clean sieve lined with double thickness of dampened cheesecloth into clean container. Thoroughly wash and dry original container, or have ready a second clean glass or ceramic container. Set funnel or coffee cone containing dampened filter paper or coffee filter over container; slowly pour liqueur through. When liqueur is filtered to desired clarity, test for sweetness; add simple syrup to taste. Cap tightly; let age about 1 month in a cool dark place.

LEMON LIQUEUR

Also known as "Limoncello" in Italy, this liqueur has been a Mediterranean favorite for centuries.

Makes about 5 cups

Peels of 10 thick-skinned lemons
4 cups 100 proof vodka
1 cup simple syrup

Remove all of the pith from the lemon peels; slice peels very thinly. Combine sliced lemon peels and vodka in a 2-quart glass or ceramic container; stir to mix. Cap tightly, or cover tightly with plastic wrap. Let liqueur steep in a cool dark place for 4 weeks, swirling mixture around in container every 3 days.

Strain liquid through clean sieve lined with double thickness of dampened cheesecloth into clean container. Thoroughly wash and dry original container, or have ready a second clean glass or ceramic container. Set funnel or coffee cone containing dampened filter paper or coffee filter over container; slowly pour liqueur through. When liqueur is filtered to desired clarity, add simple syrup. Cap tightly; let age about 1 month in a cool dark place.

TIP: Serve this liqueur directly from the freezer for that truly European experience.

LEMON LIME LIQUEUR

By adjusting the amount of lemons and limes you
use in this recipe, you can make some interesting variations.

Makes about 4 cups

3 large lemons, sliced
3 large limes, sliced
3 cups vodka
1 cup simple syrup

Combine sliced lemons, sliced limes, and vodka in a 2-quart glass or ceramic container; stir to mix. Cap tightly, or cover tightly with plastic wrap. Let liqueur steep in a cool dark place for 3 weeks, swirling mixture around in container every 3 days.

Strain liquid through clean sieve lined with double thickness of dampened cheesecloth into clean container. Thoroughly wash and dry original container, or have ready a second clean glass or ceramic container. Set funnel or coffee cone containing dampened filter paper or coffee filter over container; slowly pour liqueur through. When liqueur is filtered to desired clarity, add simple syrup. Cap tightly; let age about 1 month in a cool dark place.

LICORICE ROOT LIQUEUR

This liqueur, when finished, should be completely clear.

Makes about 4 cups

3 tablespoons chopped fresh licorice root
3 cups vodka
1 cup simple syrup
1 tablespoon glycerin

Combine chopped licorice root and vodka in a 2-quart glass or ceramic container; stir to mix. Cap tightly, or cover tightly with plastic wrap. Let liqueur steep in a cool dark place for 3 weeks, swirling mixture around in container every 3 days.

Strain liquid through clean sieve lined with double thickness of dampened cheesecloth into clean container. Thoroughly wash and dry original container, or have ready a second clean glass or ceramic container. Set funnel or coffee cone containing dampened filter paper or coffee filter over container; slowly pour liqueur through. When liqueur is filtered to desired clarity, add simple syrup and glycerin; stir to combine. Cap tightly; let age about 1 month in a cool dark place.

LIQUEUR AU CHOCOLAT

Chocolate lovers will adore this rich
and decadent liqueur.

Makes about 3 cups

1 cup Simple Syrup
3 cups vodka
1 vanilla bean, split
5 tablespoons unsweetened cocoa powder,
preferably Dutch process

Combine vodka, 1 cup simple syrup, the cocoa powder, and vanilla bean in a 2-quart glass or ceramic container. Cap tightly or cover tightly with plastic wrap. Let steep in a cool dark place 2 weeks, shaking thoroughly every 2 days.

Strain liqueur through sieve lined with double thickness of dampened cheesecloth into a clean container. Thoroughly wash and dry original container, or have ready second clean glass or ceramic container. Set funnel or coffee cone containing filter paper or coffee filter over container; slowly pour liqueur through (the residue of the cocoa powder will be very thick, so filter papers may have to be changed twice or more in middle of process. Let mixture drip overnight, if necessary.) When liqueur is filtered to desired clarity, test for sweetness. Adjust sweetening to taste with additional simple syrup, if desired, then cover tightly and let liqueur age 4 weeks in a cool dark place.

TIP: If this recipe is too chocolaty for you, add equal parts of vodka and simple syrup until desired flavor is obtained.

MANGO BRANDY

Use only the ripest mangoes for this recipe.
Under ripe fruit will produce an inferior product.

Makes about 4 cups

4 large ripe mangoes
2 cups brandy
1 1/2 cups Simple Syrup

Wash and rinse mangoes; peel mangoes, slicing fruit in half lengthwise; remove pits; cut into large pieces. Combine mangoes and brandy in a 2-quart glass or ceramic container; add simple syrup; stir to mix. Cap tightly, or cover tightly with plastic wrap. Let cordial steep in a cool dark place for 8 weeks, swirling mixture around in container once a week.

Strain cordial through sieve lined with double thickness of dampened cheesecloth into clean container. Thoroughly wash and dry original container, or have ready a second clean glass or ceramic container. Set funnel or coffee cone lined with dampened filter paper or coffee filter over container; slowly pour cordial through. When cordial is filtered to desired clarity, test for sweetness; add additional simple syrup to taste. Cover tightly; let age 2 to 4 weeks in a cool dark place.

MAPLE LIQUEUR

You will not believe the flavor of
this easy to make liqueur.

Makes about 4 cups

2 cups pure maple syrup
2 cups Canadian whisky

Combine maple syrup and Canadian whisky in a 2-quart glass or ceramic container; stir to mix. Cap tightly, or cover tightly with plastic wrap. Let liqueur steep in a cool dark place for 3 weeks, swirling mixture around in container every 3 days.

There should be no need to filter or strain this liqueur after the aging process. However, depending on the quality of the maple syrup you use, the final product may be a little cloudy. This should not effect the overall taste.

MARSALA CREAM

Marsala wine is produced in Italy, and is predominately used in cooking.

Makes about 5 cups

**1 1/2 cups Simple Syrup
5 egg yolks
1 cup half-and-half
1 1/2 cups vodka
1/2 cup dry Marsala
1 teaspoon vanilla extract
1 cinnamon stick**

  Beat egg yolks lightly in top of double boiler; slowly blend in half-and-half. Set over simmering water; cook, stirring constantly, until mixture thickens slightly, about 5 minutes. Remove from heat; strain through sieve lined with double thickness of dampened cheesecloth into heatproof 2-quart glass or ceramic container. Stir in 1 1/2 cups simple syrup, or to taste; let cool to room temperature.

  Add vodka, Marsala, and vanilla extract to cooled mixture. Pour mixture through funnel into clean bottles or jars, adding a one-inch piece of cinnamon stick in each. Cap tightly; store in a cool dark place about 6 weeks, shaking 2 or 3 times a week until there is no separation.

MEXICAN COFFEE CORDIAL

This recipe will produce a much richer and flavorful cordial than the Coffee Liqueur recipe.

Makes about 4 cups

3 cups Simple Syrup
6 tablespoons instant coffee
6 tablespoons boiling water
1 vanilla bean, split
15 whole cloves
10 whole allspice
2 pieces (1 inch each) cinnamon stick
2 cups brandy

Pour boiling water over instant coffee in medium saucepan; stir to dissolve. Add 3 cups simple syrup, the vanilla bean, cloves, allspice, and cinnamon stick; heat over medium flame to boiling. Remove from heat; let cool to room temperature.

Pour cooled mixture into a 2-quart glass or ceramic container; add brandy, stirring to combine. Cap tightly or cover tightly with plastic wrap. Let steep 2 weeks in a cool dark place, swirling mixture around in container every 3 days.

Strain cordial through sieve lined with double thickness of dampened cheesecloth into clean container. Thoroughly wash and dry original container, or have ready a second clean glass or ceramic container. Set funnel or coffee cone lined with dampened filter paper or coffee filter over container; slowly pour cordial through. When cordial is filtered to desired clarity, test for sweetness. Adjust sweetening to taste with additional simple syrup, then cover tightly and let cordial age 3 to 4 weeks in a cool dark place.

TIP: 1 tablespoon vanilla extract may be substituted for the split vanilla bean.

MINT CREAM CORDIAL

You can use either the Spearmint Liqueur or
Creme de Menthe recipe to make this
wonderful cordial.

Makes about 5 cups

1 14 ounce can sweetened condensed milk
1 1/4 cup mint liqueur
1 cup whipping cream
4 eggs

Combine sweetened condensed milk, mint liqueur, whipping cream, and eggs in a blender. Process at medium speed for approximately 1 minute. Transfer cordial to an air- tight glass or ceramic container; cap tightly. Let cordial age in the refrigerator overnight before using.

TIP: This cordial can be stored for up to 1 month. Refrigerate any unused portion.

MINT JULEP

Fresh Mint Juleps are the traditional cocktail of the Kentucky Derby.

Makes about 4 cups

1 cup Simple Syrup
3 cups bourbon
1 cup fresh peppermint leaves

Coarsely chop the peppermint leaves with a sharp knife. Pour the chopped leaves into a 2-quart glass or ceramic container; add simple syrup and bourbon; stir. Cap the container tightly, or cover tightly with plastic wrap. Let mixture steep for at least 4 weeks, swirling mixture in container every 3 days.

Drain mixture in medium-mesh sieve set over 4-cup measure, pressing with the back of a large spoon to extract as much liquid as possible; discard contents of sieve. Strain liquid through clean sieve lined with double thickness of dampened cheesecloth into clean container. Thoroughly wash and dry original container, or have ready a second clean glass or ceramic container. Set funnel or coffee cone containing dampened filter paper or coffee filter over container; slowly pour liqueur through. When liqueur if filtered to desired clarity, test for sweetness; add simple syrup to taste. Cap tightly; let age about 1 month in a cool dark place.

TIP: 3 tablespoons of peppermint extract may be substituted for the fresh leaves, however, the flavor and quality will not be the same.

NECTARINE LIQUEUR

Here is a nice refreshing liqueur that
has a softer flavor than oranges.

Makes about 4 cups

6 large nectarines, sliced and pitted
3 cup vodka
1 cup simple syrup

  Combine sliced nectarines and vodka in a 2-quart glass or ceramic container; stir to mix. Cap tightly, or cover tightly with plastic wrap. Let liqueur steep in a cool dark place for 3 weeks, swirling mixture around in container every 3 days.

  Strain liquid through clean sieve lined with double thickness of dampened cheesecloth into clean container. Thoroughly wash and dry original container, or have ready a second clean glass or ceramic container. Set funnel or coffee cone containing dampened filter paper or coffee filter over container; slowly pour liqueur through. When liqueur is filtered to desired clarity, add simple syrup; stir to combine. Cap tightly; let age about 1 month in a cool dark place.

TIP: Make sure you remove all of the seeds from the nectarines prior to steeping. The pits will give your liqueur a bitter flavor.

ORANGE & SPICE BRANDY

Once you have enjoyed this fragrant liqueur,
you will want to make it over and over again.

Makes about 4 cups

4 medium oranges, sliced and pitted
1 1/2 teaspoons pure orange extract
1/2 teaspoon ground cinnamon
1/2 teaspoon caraway seeds
1/2 teaspoon coriander
3 cups brandy
1 cup simple syrup

Combine sliced oranges, orange extract, ground cinnamon, caraway seeds, coriander and brandy in a 2-quart glass or ceramic container; stir to mix. Cap tightly, or cover tightly with plastic wrap. Let liqueur steep in a cool dark place for 3 weeks, swirling mixture around in container every 3 days.

Strain liquid through clean sieve lined with double thickness of dampened cheesecloth into clean container. Thoroughly wash and dry original container, or have ready a second clean glass or ceramic container. Set funnel or coffee cone containing dampened filter paper or coffee filter over container; slowly pour liqueur through. When liqueur is filtered to desired clarity, add simple syrup; stir to combine. Cap tightly; let age about 1 month in a cool dark place.

TIP: Make sure you remove all of the seeds from the oranges prior to steeping. The pits will give your liqueur a bitter flavor.

ORANGE LIQUEUR

For a slightly different flavor, try this recipe
using tangerines or tangelos.

Makes about 4 cups

3 large oranges
3 cups brandy
1 cup honey

  Peel oranges, removing inner white pith from rind; reserve orange pulp for other use. Cut peels into 2 inch by 1/4 inch strips. Combine orange peels and brandy in a 2-quart glass or ceramic container; cap tightly, or cover tightly with plastic wrap. Let liqueur steep in a cool dark place for 3 weeks, swirling mixture around in container every 3 days.

  Remove orange peels; add honey; stir. Let liqueur set for 3 more days. Strain liqueur through sieve lined with double thickness of dampened cheesecloth into clean container. Thoroughly wash and dry original container, or have ready a second clean glass or ceramic container. Set funnel or coffee cone lined with dampened filter paper or coffee filter over container; slowly pour liqueur through. Store in an air-tight container.

ORANGE CREAM CORDIAL

Using the Orange Liqueur from the previous recipe,
try making this cordial for a delicious treat.

Makes about 5 cups

**1 14 ounce can sweetened condensed milk
1 1/4 cup orange liqueur
1 cup whipping cream
4 eggs**

Combine sweetened condensed milk, orange liqueur, whipping cream, and eggs in a blender. Process at medium speed for approximately 1 minute. Transfer cordial to an air- tight glass or ceramic container; cap tightly. Let cordial age in the refrigerator overnight before using.

TIP: This cordial can be stored for up to 1 month. Refrigerate any unused portion.

ORANGE SHERRY

This is a wonderful cordial to enjoy
with friends after a fine dinner.

Makes about 4 cups

**2 medium oranges
4 cups dry sherry**

Peel oranges, removing inner white pith from rind; reserve orange pulp for other use. Cut peels into 2 inch by 1/4 inch strips. Combine orange peels and sherry in a 2-quart glass or ceramic container; cap tightly, or cover tightly with plastic wrap. Let liqueur steep in a cool dark place for 4 weeks, swirling mixture around in container every 3 days.

Strain liqueur through sieve lined with double thickness of dampened cheesecloth into clean container. Thoroughly wash and dry original container, or have ready a second clean glass or ceramic container. Set funnel or coffee cone lined with dampened filter paper or coffee filter over container; slowly pour liqueur through. Store in an air-tight container. Cover tightly; let age 4 weeks in a cool dark place.

PAPAYA CORDIAL

This light cordial is certain to stir thoughts
of a beautiful sun-drenched tropical island.

Makes about 4 cups

3 large ripe papayas
1 cup Simple Syrup
1 1/4 cups light rum

Wash and rinse papayas; peel papayas, slice fruit in half lengthwise, and scoop out seeds; cut into large pieces. Combine papayas and rum in a 2-quart glass or ceramic container; add simple syrup; stir to mix. Cap tightly, or cover tightly with plastic wrap. Let cordial steep in a cool dark place for 8 weeks, swirling mixture around in container once a week.

Strain cordial through sieve lined with double thickness of dampened cheesecloth into clean container. Thoroughly wash and dry original container, or have ready a second clean glass or ceramic container. Set funnel or coffee cone lined with dampened filter paper or coffee filter over container; slowly pour cordial through. When cordial is filtered to desired clarity, test for sweetness; add additional simple syrup to taste. Cover tightly; let age 2 to 4 weeks in a cool dark place.

PEACH BRANDY

Once you taste this easy-to-make cordial, it will certainly become one of your favorites.

Makes about 6 cups

2 pounds ripe, soft peaches
2 cups brandy
2 cups Simple Syrup

Wash and rinse peaches; slice peaches, unpeeled, into large pieces, removing pits. Combine peaches and brandy in a 2-quart glass or ceramic container; add simple syrup; stir to mix. Cap tightly, or cover tightly with plastic wrap. Let cordial steep in a cool dark place for 8 weeks, swirling mixture around in container once a week.

Strain cordial through sieve lined with double thickness of dampened cheesecloth into clean container. Thoroughly wash and dry original container, or have ready a second clean glass or ceramic container. Set funnel or coffee cone lined with dampened filter paper or coffee filter over container; slowly pour cordial through. When cordial is filtered to desired clarity, test for sweetness; add additional simple syrup to taste. Cover tightly; let age 2 to 4 weeks in a cool dark place.

PEACH LIQUEUR

This is a wonderful liqueur that makes the
best use of a bountiful summer harvest.

Makes about 4 cups

10 large ripe peaches, sliced and pitted
3 cups vodka
1 cup simple syrup

Combine sliced peaches, vodka, and simple syrup in a 2-quart glass or ceramic container. Cap tightly or cover tightly with plastic wrap. Let steep in a cool dark place 3 weeks, shaking thoroughly every 2 days.

Drain fruit mixture in medium-mesh sieve set over a clean glass bowl, pressing with the back of a large spoon to extract as much liquid as possible; discard contents of sieve. Strain liquid through clean sieve lined with double thickness of dampened cheesecloth into clean container. Thoroughly wash and dry original container, or have ready a second clean glass or ceramic container. Set funnel or coffee cone containing dampened filter paper or coffee filter over container; slowly pour liqueur through. When liqueur is filtered to desired clarity, test for sweetness; add simple syrup to taste. Cap tightly; let age about 1 month in a cool dark place.

TIP: After straining the liqueur from the fruit, chop up the reserved peaches and use as a delicious topping for ice cream.

PEACH VANILLA CORDIAL

This is a delightful cordial that shares
two mild and fragrant flavors.

Makes about 4 cups

10 large ripe peaches, sliced and pitted
3 cups light rum
1 1/2 teaspoons pure vanilla extract
1 cup simple syrup

Combine sliced peaches, light rum, vanilla extract, and simple syrup in a 2-quart glass or ceramic container. Cap tightly or cover tightly with plastic wrap. Let steep in a cool dark place 3 weeks, shaking thoroughly every 2 days.

Drain fruit mixture in medium-mesh sieve set over a clean glass bowl, pressing with the back of a large spoon to extract as much liquid as possible; discard contents of sieve. Strain liquid through clean sieve lined with double thickness of dampened cheesecloth into clean container. Thoroughly wash and dry original container, or have ready a second clean glass or ceramic container. Set funnel or coffee cone containing dampened filter paper or coffee filter over container; slowly pour liqueur through. When liqueur is filtered to desired clarity, test for sweetness; add simple syrup to taste. Cap tightly; let age about 1 month in a cool dark place.

PEAR CORDIAL

The longer the pears age during the first steeping process, the better the flavor will develop.

Makes about 4 cups

2 pounds ripe pears
2 cups Simple Syrup
2 cups vodka

Wash and rinse pears; slice pears, unpeeled, into large pieces, removing stems and seeds. Combine pears and vodka in a 2-quart glass or ceramic container; add simple syrup; stir to mix. Cap tightly, or cover tightly with plastic wrap. Let cordial steep in a cool dark place for 10 weeks, swirling mixture around in container once a week.

Strain cordial through sieve lined with double thickness of dampened cheesecloth into clean container. Thoroughly wash and dry original container, or have ready a second clean glass or ceramic container. Set funnel or coffee cone lined with dampened filter paper or coffee filter over container; slowly pour cordial through. When cordial is filtered to desired clarity, test for sweetness; add additional simple syrup to taste. Cover tightly; let age 2 to 4 weeks in a cool dark place.

PEPPERMINT SCHNAPPS LIQUEUR

This is an easy and inexpensive way to make a nice liqueur to warm you on cold winter nights.

Makes about 5 cups

1/2 cup sugar
2 cups light corn syrup
2 cups vodka
2 teaspoons pure peppermint extract

In a medium saucepan, combine sugar and corn syrup. Heat over a very low flame, stirring constantly. Bring to a slow simmer, taking care not to scorch the syrup. Remove from heat when the sugar has melted. Let cool.

Transfer mixture to a large glass or ceramic container. Add vodka and peppermint extract; stir to mix. Cap tightly or cover tightly with plastic wrap. Age in a cool, dark place for at least 2 weeks. Shake gently each day. There should be no need to filter or strain this liqueur after the aging process.

PEPPER VODKA

Served at room temperature, small draughts of this liqueur will certainly warm the soul on those cold winter evenings.

Makes about 6 cups

5 cups vodka
6 large hot red chili peppers
1/2 cup Simple Syrup

Slice chili peppers lengthwise into 2 inch by 1/4 inch strips, using caution not to get oils or juices in your eyes. Combine chili peppers (including seeds) and vodka in a 2-quart glass or ceramic container; add simple syrup; stir to mix. Cap tightly, or cover tightly with plastic wrap. Let liqueur steep in a cool dark place for 3 weeks, swirling mixture around in container every 3 days.

Remove peels. Strain liqueur through sieve lined with double thickness of dampened cheesecloth into clean container. Thoroughly wash and dry original container, or have ready a second clean glass or ceramic container. Set funnel or coffee cone lined with dampened filter paper or coffee filter over container; slowly pour liqueur through. Store in an air-tight container.

PINA COLADA CREAM LIQUEUR

This tropical concoction is perfect on hot summer afternoons.

Makes about 4 cups

**1 cup fresh pineapple, chopped
1 cup vodka
2 cups light rum
1 cup canned cream of coconut
1/2 cup sweetened condensed milk
1/2 cup evaporated milk
2 teaspoons coconut extract**

Combine pineapple, light rum, and vodka in a 2-quart glass or ceramic container. Cap tightly or cover tightly with plastic wrap. Let steep in a cool dark place 2 weeks, shaking thoroughly every 2 days.

Drain fruit mixture in medium-mesh sieve set over a clean glass bowl, pressing with the back of a large spoon to extract as much liquid as possible; discard contents of sieve.

In a clean blender, combine the liqueur with the cream of coconut, the sweetened condensed milk, the evaporated milk, and the coconut extract. Process on medium until all ingredients are blended thoroughly. Refrigerate liqueur. Serve cold.

This liqueur should remain refrigerated, and is best if consumed within 1 week.

PINEAPPLE LIQUEUR

Pour some of this Pineapple Liqueur in a blender, and combine with a bit of coconut syrup and a few ice cubes for an authentic tropical treat.

Makes about 3 to 3 1/2 cups

1 cup Simple Syrup
2 1/2 cups coarsely chopped fresh pineapple
1 1/2 cups dark rum
1 1/2 cups light rum
1 vanilla bean, split

Combine pineapple, dark and light rum, and vanilla bean in a 2-quart glass or ceramic container. Cap tightly or cover tightly with plastic wrap. Let steep in a cool dark place 3 weeks, swirling mixture around in container every three days.

Drain pineapple in a coarse sieve set over 4-cup measure, pressing fruit with the back of a large spoon to extract as much liquid as possible; discard contents of sieve. Strain liquid through clean sieve lined with double thickness of dampened cheesecloth into clean container. Thoroughly wash and dry original 2-quart container, or have second clean glass or ceramic container. Set funnel or coffee cone containing dampened filter paper or coffee filter over container; slowly pour liqueur through. When liqueur is filtered to desired clarity, test for sweetness; add simple syrup to taste. Cover tightly; let age 4 to 6 weeks in a cool dark place.

PLUM CORDIAL

Use the darkest plums available to give this cordial a beautiful purple color.

Makes about 8 cups

3 pounds ripe plums
2 cups sugar
6 cups vodka

Wash and rinse plums; slice plums into large pieces, removing pits. Combine plums and sugar in a 2-quart glass or ceramic container; add vodka; stir to mix. Cap tightly, or cover tightly with plastic wrap. Let cordial steep in a cool dark place for 3 weeks, swirling mixture around in container every 3 days.

Strain cordial through sieve lined with double thickness of dampened cheesecloth into clean container. Thoroughly wash and dry original container, or have ready a second clean glass or ceramic container. Set funnel or coffee cone lined with dampened filter paper or coffee filter over container; slowly pour cordial through. When cordial is filtered to desired clarity, test for sweetness; add additional simple syrup to taste. Cover tightly; let age 2 to 4 months in a cool dark place.

TIP: For a smoother cordial, brandy may be substituted for the vodka.

PLUM RUM

This variation of the previous recipe produces a truly unique flavor, and a mellower finish.

Makes about 4 cups

3 pounds fresh, ripe plums
2 cups sugar
2 cups water
3 cups white rum
Simple Syrup

Thoroughly wash and rinse plums; slice plums in half, removing pits. In a medium saucepan, combine plums, water, and sugar. Bring to a slow simmer over a low heat, stirring constantly. After ingredients come to a full boil, continue to cook 5 minutes. Remove from heat; let cool to room temperature.

Pour cordial mixture into a 2-quart glass or ceramic container; add rum. Cap tightly, or cover tightly with plastic wrap. Let cordial steep in a cool dark place for 4 weeks, swirling mixture around in container once a week.

Strain cordial through sieve lined with double thickness of dampened cheesecloth into clean container. Thoroughly wash and dry original container, or have ready a second clean glass or ceramic container. Set funnel or coffee cone lined with dampened filter paper or coffee filter over container; slowly pour cordial through. When cordial is filtered to desired clarity, test for sweetness. Adjust sweetness by adding simple syrup. Store in an air-tight container

POMEGRANATE LIQUEUR

If you have pomegranates available, this
is certainly a recipe you should try.

Makes about 5 cups

2 large pomegranates
Peel of 1 lemon, thinly sliced
3 cups vodka
2 cups simple syrup

Remove the pods from the pomegranates, discarding the pith and skins. Place the pods in a glass or ceramic bowl. With a slotted metal spoon, gently crush the pods to release as much of the juice as possible. Be careful not to pulverize the seeds; they will add a bitter flavor to your liqueur.

Combine mashed pomegranates, lemon peel, vodka, and simple syrup in a 2-quart glass or ceramic container. Cap tightly or cover tightly with plastic wrap. Let steep in a cool dark place 4 weeks, shaking thoroughly every 2 days.

Drain fruit mixture in medium-mesh sieve set over a clean glass bowl, pressing with the back of a large spoon to extract as much liquid as possible; discard contents of sieve. Strain liquid through clean sieve lined with double thickness of dampened cheesecloth into clean container. Thoroughly wash and dry original container, or have ready a second clean glass or ceramic container. Set funnel or coffee cone containing dampened filter paper or coffee filter over container; slowly pour liqueur through. When liqueur is filtered to desired clarity, test for sweetness; add simple syrup to taste. Cap tightly; let age about 1 month in a cool dark place.

TIP: For the best results, you want to use pomegranates that are at the peak of ripeness. Under ripe and over ripe fruit will result in a less than perfect product.

PRUNE CORDIAL

This unusual cordial has a delicious flavor
like nothing you've ever tasted.

Makes about 4 cups

1 pound dried prunes
4 cups water
4 cups whiskey
2 tablespoons sugar
Simple Syrup

Combine prunes and water in a medium saucepan; bring prunes to a slow boil over a medium flame; reduce heat, let simmer five minutes; drain prunes, discarding water. Combine prunes, whiskey, and sugar in a 2-quart glass or ceramic container; stir to mix. Cap tightly, or cover tightly with plastic wrap. Let cordial steep in a cool dark place for 2 weeks, swirling mixture around in container every 3 days.

Strain cordial through sieve lined with double thickness of dampened cheesecloth into clean container. Thoroughly wash and dry original container, or have ready a second clean glass or ceramic container. Set funnel or coffee cone lined with dampened filter paper or coffee filter over container; slowly pour liqueur through. When liqueur is filtered to desired clarity, test for sweetness; add simple syrup to taste. Cover tightly; let age 4 weeks in a cool dark place.

PUMPKIN PIE LIQUEUR

You will not believe the flavor of this liqueur.

Makes about 5 cups

1 1/2 lbs. fresh pumpkin, cut into small cubes
3 cups water
Peel of 1 lemon, sliced and pith removed
Juice of 1 lemon
3 cups light rum
1 teaspoon ground cinnamon
1 teaspoon ground allspice
1/2 teaspoon ground dried ginger
1 cup simple syrup

In a medium saucepan, combine pumpkin, water, lemon peel, and lemon juice. Heat over a low flame, stirring constantly. Bring to a slow simmer, cooking until the pumpkin is soft, about 30 minutes. Remove from heat. Let cool.

Transfer mixture (including any remaining liquid) to a large glass or ceramic container. Add rum, cinnamon, allspice, and ginger; stir to mix. Cap tightly or cover tightly with plastic wrap. Age in a cool, dark place for at least 3 weeks. Shake gently each day.

Drain mixture in medium-mesh sieve set over 4-cup measure, pressing with the back of a large spoon to extract as much liquid as possible; discard contents of sieve. Strain liquid through clean sieve lined with double thickness of dampened cheesecloth into clean container. Thoroughly wash and dry original container, or have ready a second clean glass or ceramic container. Set funnel or coffee cone containing dampened filter paper or coffee filter over container; slowly pour liqueur through. When liqueur if filtered to desired clarity, add simple syrup. Cap tightly; let age about 1 more month in a cool dark place.

RAISIN & WINE LIQUEUR

The combination of raisins, white wine, and spices
give this liqueur a very unusual and exotic flavor.

Makes about 4 cups

1/2 cup black raisins
Juice of 1 lemon
1 cinnamon stick, broken
1 1/2 cups dry white wine
1 1/2 cups light rum
1/4 teaspoon ground ginger
1/4 teaspoon ground cloves
1 teaspoon fresh lemon zest
1 cup simple syrup
1 cup honey

Combine black raisins, lemon juice, cinnamon stick, white wine, light rum, ground ginger, ground cloves, and lemon zest in a 2-quart glass or ceramic container; stir to mix. Cap tightly, or cover tightly with plastic wrap. Let liqueur steep in a cool dark place for 3 weeks, swirling mixture around in container every 3 days.

Strain liquid through clean sieve lined with double thickness of dampened cheesecloth into clean container. Thoroughly wash and dry original container, or have ready a second clean glass or ceramic container. Set funnel or coffee cone containing dampened filter paper or coffee filter over container; slowly pour liqueur through. When liqueur is filtered to desired clarity, add simple syrup and honey; stir to combine. Cap tightly; let age about 1 month in a cool dark place.

RASPBERRY BRANDY

This is one of those cordials that
tastes better the longer it ages.

Makes about 5 cups

4 cups fresh red raspberries, slightly crushed
3 cups brandy
1 cup simple syrup
1 teaspoon glycerin

Combine crushed raspberries, brandy, and simple syrup in a 2-quart glass or ceramic container. Cap tightly or cover tightly with plastic wrap. Let steep in a cool dark place 6 weeks, shaking thoroughly once a week.

Drain fruit mixture in medium-mesh sieve set over a clean glass bowl, pressing with the back of a large spoon to extract as much liquid as possible; discard contents of sieve. Strain liquid through clean sieve lined with double thickness of dampened cheesecloth into clean container. Thoroughly wash and dry original container, or have ready a second clean glass or ceramic container. Set funnel or coffee cone containing dampened filter paper or coffee filter over container; slowly pour liqueur through. When liqueur is filtered to desired clarity, test for sweetness; add simple syrup to taste. Add glycerin and stir to mix. Cap tightly; let age about 2 more months in a cool dark place.

RASPBERRY LIQUEUR

The longer the raspberries steep during the initial aging process, the darker the color of the finished product will be.

Makes about 3 cups

**12 ounces fresh raspberries
1 cup vodka
1/2 cup brandy
1/4 cup Simple Syrup**

Thoroughly wash raspberries under cold running water. Place raspberries, vodka, brandy, and simple syrup in a 2-quart glass or ceramic container; cap tightly or cover tightly with plastic wrap. Let mixture steep for 2 weeks, swirling contents of container every 3 days.

Strain liqueur through a fine sieve set over 4-cup measure, pressing fruit with the back of a large spoon to extract as much liquid as possible; discard contents of sieve. Strain liquid through clean sieve lined with double thickness of dampened cheesecloth into clean container. Thoroughly wash and dry original 2-quart container, or have second clean glass or ceramic container. Set funnel or coffee cone containing dampened filter paper or coffee filter over container; slowly pour liqueur through. When liqueur is filtered to desired clarity, test for sweetness; add simple syrup to taste. Cover tightly; let age 2 to 4 weeks in a cool dark place.

RUM CREAM LIQUEUR

Served ice cold, or poured over a scoop of ice cream, this liqueur can be enjoyed any time of the year.

Makes about 4 cups

1 1/2 cups dark rum
1 cup sweetened condensed milk
1 egg
1 teaspoon vanilla extract

Combine all ingredients in a clean blender; process on high for approximately 1 minute. Transfer liqueur to a large glass or ceramic container; cap tightly or cover tightly with plastic wrap. For best flavor, allow liqueur to stand in the refrigerator overnight or up to 2 weeks before serving.

TIP: To prevent spoilage, keep liqueur refrigerated.

RUM SHRUB

Here is another English-style shrub.
This one is delightfully refreshing
served ice cold.

Makes about 6 cups

6 medium oranges, thinly sliced
4 cups light rum
2 cups fresh orange juice
Peel of 1 lemon, sliced, pith removed
4 cups sugar

Combine sliced oranges, rum, 1 cup of the orange juice, lemon peel and sugar in a 2-quart glass or ceramic container. Stir until the sugar has completely dissolved. Cap tightly, or cover tightly with plastic wrap. Let cordial steep in a cool dark place for 2 weeks, swirling mixture around in container every 3 days.

Remove peels and orange slices. Strain cordial through sieve lined with double thickness of dampened cheesecloth into clean container. Thoroughly wash and dry original container, or have ready a second clean glass or ceramic container. Set funnel or coffee cone lined with dampened filter paper or coffee filter over container; slowly pour cordial through. When cordial is filtered to desired clarity, test for sweetness; add simple syrup to taste. Add additional cup of fresh orange juice. Cover tightly and let cordial age for an additional 2 to 4 weeks.

SAGE & LEMON LIQUEUR

Here is another unusual but fragrant liqueur
that combines fresh herbs and fruit.

Makes about 4 cups

12 fresh sage leaves, slightly chopped
Peel of 1 lemon, sliced thinly, pith removed
1 1/2 cups dry white wine
1 1/2 cups vodka
Juice of 1 lemon
1 whole clove
6 white raisins
1 cup simple syrup

Combine chopped sage leaves, sliced lemon peel, white wine, vodka, lemon juice, whole clove, and raisins in a 2-quart glass or ceramic container; stir to mix. Cap tightly, or cover tightly with plastic wrap. Let liqueur steep in a cool dark place for 3 weeks, swirling mixture around in container every 3 days.

Strain liquid through clean sieve lined with double thickness of dampened cheesecloth into clean container. Thoroughly wash and dry original container, or have ready a second clean glass or ceramic container. Set funnel or coffee cone containing dampened filter paper or coffee filter over container; slowly pour liqueur through. When liqueur is filtered to desired clarity, add simple syrup; stir to combine. Cap tightly; let age about 1 month in a cool dark place.

SCOTTISH HIGHLAND LIQUEUR

This delicious liqueur has been made for generations in the Highlands of Scotland.

Makes about 5 cups

4 cups Scotch
1 1/2 cups honey
2 teaspoons dried Angelica root, chopped
1/4 teaspoon crushed fennel seeds
2 medium lemons

Peel lemons, removing inner white pith from rind; reserve lemon pulp for other use. Cut peels into 2 inch by 1/4 inch strips. Combine lemon peels, Scotch, honey, Angelica root, and fennel seed in a 2-quart glass or ceramic container; cap tightly, or cover tightly with plastic wrap. Shake or stir mixture several times in the first 24 hours; after first day, remove lemon peels from liqueur and recover. Let steep 2 weeks, stirring or shaking container every other day.

Strain liqueur through sieve lined with double thickness of dampened cheesecloth into clean container. Thoroughly wash and dry original container, or have ready a second clean glass or ceramic container. Set funnel or coffee cone lined with dampened filter paper or coffee filter over container; slowly pour liqueur through. Store in an air-tight container. Cover tightly; let age 6 months in a cool dark place.

TIP: Use a good quality Scotch to produce a finer finished liqueur.

SLOE GIN

Sloe berries are a member of the plum family.

Makes about 6 cups

**1 pound fresh sloe berries
4 cups gin
6 large almonds, chopped
1 1/2 cups Simple Syrup**

Wash and drain sloes, removing any stems and stalks; crush berries with the back of a large spoon. Combine crushed sloes, gin, chopped almonds, and simple syrup in a 2-quart glass or ceramic container; stir to mix. Cap tightly, or cover tightly with plastic wrap. Let cordial steep in a cool dark place for 8 weeks, swirling mixture around in container weekly.

Strain cordial through sieve lined with double thickness of dampened cheesecloth into clean container. Thoroughly wash and dry original container, or have ready a second clean glass or ceramic container. Set funnel or coffee cone lined with dampened filter paper or coffee filter over container; slowly pour cordial through. When cordial is filtered to desired clarity, test for sweetness; add additional simple syrup to taste. Cover tightly; let age 4 weeks in a cool dark place.

TIP: Sloe berries grow in the wild, and are often available at fruit stands and farmer's markets.

SPEARMINT LIQUEUR

If you choose to omit the food coloring from this recipe, the finished liqueur will be practically clear.

Makes about 5 cups

1 1/2 cups fresh spearmint leaves
3 cups vodka
2 cups Simple Syrup
1 teaspoon glycerin
8 drops green food coloring (optional)
2 drops blue food coloring (optional)

Rinse spearmint leaves under cold running water. Carefully mince leaves with a sharp knife. Combine minced spearmint leaves and vodka in a 2-quart glass or ceramic container; stir to mix. Cap tightly, or cover tightly with plastic wrap. Let liqueur steep in a cool dark place for 3 weeks, swirling mixture around in container every 3 days.

Strain liqueur through sieve lined with double thickness of dampened cheesecloth into clean container. Thoroughly wash and dry original container, or have ready a second clean glass or ceramic container. Set funnel or coffee cone lined with dampened filter paper or coffee filter over container; slowly pour liqueur through. When liqueur is filtered to desired clarity, add simple syrup and glycerin; stir to mix. Add green and blue food coloring, if desired. Cover tightly; let age 2 to 4 weeks in a cool dark place.

TIP: If liqueur is not clear after final aging, you may want to re-filter. Follow the same process as before.

SPICED APPLE LIQUEUR

This delicious liqueur is wonderful on a
cool autumn evening.

Makes about 4 cups

**1 pound tart apples (about 3 medium)
2 cups Simple Syrup
2 whole cloves
1/4 teaspoon ground nutmeg
peel from 1 fresh medium lime
2 cups vodka**

Wash and rinse apples; core apples, and chop (unpeeled) into 1-inch by 1-inch pieces. Combine apples, cloves, nutmeg, lime peel, and vodka in a 2-quart glass or ceramic container; add simple syrup; stir to mix. Cap tightly, or cover tightly with plastic wrap. Let liqueur steep in a cool dark place for 8 weeks, swirling mixture around in container once a week.

Strain liqueur through sieve lined with double thickness of dampened cheesecloth into clean container. Thoroughly wash and dry original container, or have ready a second clean glass or ceramic container. Set funnel or coffee cone lined with dampened filter paper or coffee filter over container; slowly pour liqueur through. When liqueur is filtered to desired clarity, test for sweetness; add additional simple syrup to taste. Cover tightly; let age 2 to 4 weeks in a cool dark place.

SPICED RUM

Spiced rum is a favorite beverage
of many Caribbean Islands.

Makes about 5 cups

**4 cups light rum
2 teaspoons pure vanilla extract
1/4 cup packed brown sugar
1 cup simple syrup
1/4 teaspoon ground allspice**

Combine light rum, vanilla extract, brown sugar, simple syrup, and ground allspice in a 2-quart glass or ceramic container; stir until all of the brown sugar is dissolved. Cap tightly, or cover tightly with plastic wrap. Let liqueur steep in a cool dark place for 3 weeks, swirling mixture around in container every 3 days.

Strain liquid through clean sieve lined with double thickness of dampened cheesecloth into clean container. Thoroughly wash and dry original container, or have ready a second clean glass or ceramic container. Set funnel or coffee cone containing dampened filter paper or coffee filter over container; slowly pour liqueur through. Cap tightly; let age about 1 month in a cool dark place.

SPICY ORANGE CORDIAL

Try adjusting the amounts of spices you
use in this recipe to create a truly
personal cordial.

Makes about 6 cups

**6 medium oranges
2 cups vodka
1 cup brandy
1 teaspoon cinnamon
1/2 teaspoon allspice
1/2 teaspoon nutmeg
2 whole cloves
3 cups Simple Syrup**

Wash and rinse oranges well; peel oranges, removing inner white pith from rinds; reserve pulp for other use. Cut peels into 2 inch by 1/4 inch strips. Combine fruit peels, vodka, brandy, cinnamon, allspice, nutmeg, and cloves in a 2-quart glass or ceramic container; add simple syrup; stir to mix. Cap tightly, or cover tightly with plastic wrap. Let cordial steep in a cool dark place for 3 weeks, swirling mixture around in container every 3 days.

Strain cordial through sieve lined with double thickness of dampened cheesecloth into clean container. Thoroughly wash and dry original container, or have ready a second clean glass or ceramic container. Set funnel or coffee cone lined with dampened filter paper or coffee filter over container; slowly pour cordial through. When cordial is filtered to desired clarity, test for sweetness; add additional simple syrup to taste. Cover tightly; let age 2 to 4 weeks in a cool dark place.

SPICY PEAR CORDIAL

This unusual cordial is uncommonly delicious.
It will surely become one of you favorites.

Makes about 6 cups

1 cup Simple Syrup
4 firm, ripe pears
4 whole cloves
1 teaspoon allspice
1 teaspoon nutmeg
4 cups vodka

Wash and rinse pears; slice pears, unpeeled, into large pieces, removing stems and seeds. Combine pears, vodka, allspice, nutmeg, and cloves in a 2-quart glass or ceramic container; add simple syrup; stir to mix. Cap tightly, or cover tightly with plastic wrap. Let cordial steep in a cool dark place for 10 weeks, swirling mixture around in container once a week.

Strain cordial through sieve lined with double thickness of dampened cheesecloth into clean container. Thoroughly wash and dry original container, or have ready a second clean glass or ceramic container. Set funnel or coffee cone lined with dampened filter paper or coffee filter over container; slowly pour cordial through. When cordial is filtered to desired clarity, test for sweetness; add additional simple syrup to taste. Cover tightly; let age 2 to 4 weeks in a cool dark place.

STAR ANISE LIQUEUR

This is a pungent yet delicious liqueur that
is best enjoyed after a fine meal.

Makes about 4 cups

2 teaspoons star anise, broken into pieces
2 cups simple syrup
2 cups vodka

Combine star anise, simple syrup, and vodka in a 2-quart glass or ceramic container; stir to mix. Cap tightly, or cover tightly with plastic wrap. Let liqueur steep in a cool dark place for 4 weeks, swirling mixture around in container every 3 days.

Strain liquid through clean sieve lined with double thickness of dampened cheesecloth into clean container. Thoroughly wash and dry original container, or have ready a second clean glass or ceramic container. Set funnel or coffee cone containing dampened filter paper or coffee filter over container; slowly pour liqueur through. Cap tightly; let age about 1 month in a cool dark place.

STRAWBERRY LIQUEUR

This recipe produces a light and fragrant liqueur. For a richer flavor, increase the strawberries to 3 pounds.

Makes about 6 cups

2 pounds strawberries
2 cups light rum
1/4 cup fresh lemon juice
2 cups Simple Syrup
4 drops red food coloring (optional)

Wash and drain strawberries; crush berries with the back of a large spoon. Combine crushed strawberries, rum, lemon juice, and simple syrup in a 2-quart glass or ceramic container; stir to mix. Cap tightly, or cover tightly with plastic wrap. Let liqueur steep in a cool dark place for 3 weeks, swirling mixture around in container every other day.

Strain liqueur through sieve lined with double thickness of dampened cheesecloth into clean container. Thoroughly wash and dry original container, or have ready a second clean glass or ceramic container. Set funnel or coffee cone lined with dampened filter paper or coffee filter over container; slowly pour liqueur through. When liqueur is filtered to desired clarity, test for sweetness; add additional simple syrup to taste. Add red food coloring, if desired; stir. Cover tightly; let age 2 additional weeks in a cool dark place.

TIP: Frozen strawberries may be substituted for the fresh. Allow to thaw completely before using.

SWEET APPLE CORDIAL

This is a delicious cordial that will certainly take the chill away from a cool autumn evening.

Makes about 5 cups

**6 Red Delicious apples, chopped and cored
2 whole cloves
1/2 teaspoon ground cinnamon
3 cups vodka
1 1/2 cups simple syrup**

   Combine chopped apples, cloves, ground cinnamon, vodka, and simple syrup in a 2-quart glass or ceramic container. Cap tightly or cover tightly with plastic wrap. Let steep in a cool dark place 4 weeks, swirling mixture around in container every 3 days.

   Drain fruit mixture in medium-mesh sieve set over a clean glass bowl, pressing with the back of a large spoon to extract as much liquid as possible; discard contents of sieve. Strain liquid through clean sieve lined with double thickness of dampened cheesecloth into clean container. Thoroughly wash and dry original container, or have ready a second clean glass or ceramic container. Set funnel or coffee cone containing dampened filter paper or coffee filter over container; slowly pour liqueur through. When liqueur is filtered to desired clarity, test for sweetness; add simple syrup to taste. Cap tightly; let age about 1 more month in a cool dark place.

SWEET APPLE LIQUEUR

This liqueur has the taste of warm apple pie.

Makes about 4 cups

1 pound Granny Smith apples (about 3 medium)
2 cups Simple Syrup
2 whole cloves
1 teaspoon ground cinnamon
2 cups brandy

Wash and rinse apples; core apples, and chop (unpeeled) into 1-inch by 1-inch pieces. Combine apples, cloves, cinnamon, and brandy in a 2-quart glass or ceramic container; add simple syrup; stir to mix. Cap tightly, or cover tightly with plastic wrap. Let liqueur steep in a cool dark place for 8 weeks, swirling mixture around in container once a week.

Strain liqueur through sieve lined with double thickness of dampened cheesecloth into clean container. Thoroughly wash and dry original container, or have ready a second clean glass or ceramic container. Set funnel or coffee cone lined with dampened filter paper or coffee filter over container; slowly pour liqueur through. When liqueur is filtered to desired clarity, test for sweetness; add additional simple syrup to taste. Cover tightly; let age 2 to 4 weeks in a cool dark place.

TANGERINE LIQUEUR

I like this liqueur because it is sweet
and fruity, but not overpowering.

Makes about 4 cups

6 tangerines
4 whole cloves
3 cups vodka
1 cup simple syrup

Peel tangerines, removing as much of the pith from the fruit as possible; discard skins. Coarsely chop tangerines. Combine chopped tangerines, cloves, vodka, and simple syrup in a 2-quart glass or ceramic container. Cap tightly or cover tightly with plastic wrap. Let steep in a cool dark place 4 weeks, swirling mixture around in container every 3 days.

Drain fruit mixture in medium-mesh sieve set over a clean glass bowl, pressing with the back of a large spoon to extract as much liquid as possible; discard contents of sieve. Strain liquid through clean sieve lined with double thickness of dampened cheesecloth into clean container. Thoroughly wash and dry original container, or have ready a second clean glass or ceramic container. Set funnel or coffee cone containing dampened filter paper or coffee filter over container; slowly pour liqueur through. When liqueur is filtered to desired clarity, test for sweetness; add simple syrup to taste. Cap tightly; let age about 1 more month in a cool dark place.

TANGERINE-NUTMEG CORDIAL

This is a nice variation of the previous recipe, with a little bit more "kick".

Makes about 4 cups

6 tangerines
2 whole cloves
3 whole nutmegs, slightly cracked
3 cups vodka
1 cup simple syrup

Peel tangerines, removing as much of the pith from the fruit as possible; discard skins. Coarsely chop tangerines. Combine chopped tangerines, cloves, cracked nutmegs, vodka, and simple syrup in a 2-quart glass or ceramic container. Cap tightly or cover tightly with plastic wrap. Let steep in a cool dark place 4 weeks, swirling mixture around in container every 3 days.

Drain fruit mixture in medium-mesh sieve set over a clean glass bowl, pressing with the back of a large spoon to extract as much liquid as possible; discard contents of sieve. Strain liquid through clean sieve lined with double thickness of dampened cheesecloth into clean container. Thoroughly wash and dry original container, or have ready a second clean glass or ceramic container. Set funnel or coffee cone containing dampened filter paper or coffee filter over container; slowly pour liqueur through. When liqueur is filtered to desired clarity, test for sweetness; add simple syrup to taste. Cap tightly; let age about 1 more month in a cool dark place.

TART APPLE CORDIAL

This is a nice variation of the sweet apple cordial.

Makes about 5 cups

6 Granny Smith apples, chopped and cored
2 whole cloves
1/2 teaspoon ground nutmeg
1 teaspoon grated lime zest
3 cups vodka
1 1/2 cups simple syrup

  Combine chopped apples, cloves, ground nutmeg, lime zest, vodka, and simple syrup in a 2-quart glass or ceramic container. Cap tightly or cover tightly with plastic wrap. Let steep in a cool dark place 4 weeks, swirling mixture around in container every 3 days.

  Drain fruit mixture in medium-mesh sieve set over a clean glass bowl, pressing with the back of a large spoon to extract as much liquid as possible; discard contents of sieve. Strain liquid through clean sieve lined with double thickness of dampened cheesecloth into clean container. Thoroughly wash and dry original container, or have ready a second clean glass or ceramic container. Set funnel or coffee cone containing dampened filter paper or coffee filter over container; slowly pour liqueur through. When liqueur is filtered to desired clarity, test for sweetness; add simple syrup to taste. Cap tightly; let age about 1 more month in a cool dark place.

VANILLA-COFFEE LIQUEUR

This is a nice and easy to make liqueur that is delicious mixed with a little fresh cream.

Makes about 4 cups

**1 1/2 cups packed brown sugar
1 cup white granulated sugar
2 cups water
1/2 cup instant coffee
3 cups vodka
1 whole vanilla bean, split**

In a medium saucepan, combine brown sugar, white sugar, and water. Heat over a low flame, stirring constantly. Bring to a slow simmer, cooking until all of the sugars have melted, taking care not to burn the mixture. Stir in the instant coffee, and continue simmering for about 2 minutes. Remove from heat. Let cool.

Transfer mixture to a large glass or ceramic container. Add vodka and split vanilla bean; stir to mix. Cap tightly or cover tightly with plastic wrap. Age in a cool, dark place for at least 3 weeks. Shake gently each day.

Strain liquid through clean sieve lined with double thickness of dampened cheesecloth into clean container. Thoroughly wash and dry original container, or have ready a second clean glass or ceramic container. Set funnel or coffee cone containing dampened filter paper or coffee filter over container; slowly pour liqueur through. Cap tightly; let age about 1 month in a cool dark place.

VANILLA LIQUEUR

Serve this liqueur as an after-dinner treat with you favorite desert.

Makes about 3 cups

**3 vanilla beans
2 cups brandy
1 cup sugar
Simple Syrup**

Split vanilla beans in half; cut into 2-inch pieces. Combine vanilla bean pieces, brandy, and sugar in a 2-quart glass or ceramic container; stir until all sugar is dissolved. Cap tightly, or cover tightly with plastic wrap. Let cordial steep in a cool dark place for 4 weeks, swirling mixture around in container once a week.

Strain cordial through sieve lined with double thickness of dampened cheesecloth into clean container. Thoroughly wash and dry original container, or have ready a second clean glass or ceramic container. Set funnel or coffee cone lined with dampened filter paper or coffee filter over container; slowly pour cordial through. When cordial is filtered to desired clarity, test for sweetness. Adjust sweetness by adding simple syrup. Cover tightly; let age 4 weeks in a cool dark place.

TIP: 1/4 cup vanilla extract may be substituted for the vanilla beans, but the flavor and quality will not be as good.

VERY BERRY BRANDY

Use a single kind of berry, or combine
varieties for a multi-berried brew.

Makes about 4 cups

1 cup Simple Syrup
5 cups fresh blueberries, raspberries,
blackberries, or strawberries, or a
combination
3 cups brandy
2 teaspoons grated orange zest
2 teaspoon grated lemon zest
10 whole allspice
5 whole cloves

If using blueberries, pierce with a fork. Combine berries, brandy, simple syrup, the orange and lemon zest, allspice, and cloves in a 2-quart glass or ceramic container. Cap tightly with plastic wrap. Let steep 2 weeks in a cool dark place, swirling mixture around in container every 3 days.

Drain berries in a coarse sieve set over 4-cup measure, pressing gently with the back of a large spoon to extract as much liquid as possible.

Strain brandy through clean sieve lined with double thickness of dampened cheesecloth into a clean container. Thoroughly wash and dry original 2-quart container, or have ready a second container. Set funnel or coffee cone containing dampened filter paper or coffee filter over container; slowly pour brandy through. When brandy is filtered to desired clarity, test for sweetness. Adjust sweetness to taste with additional simple syrup, if desired.
Cover tightly; let brandy age 3 to 4 weeks in a cool dark place.

TIP: An equivalent amount of frozen berries can be substituted for the fresh. Defrost completely before using.

VIN DE CERISE
(CHERRY-INFUSED WINE)

French in origin, this aperitif is wonderful served prior to dinner.

Makes about 5 cups

1 pound sweet, ripe cherries
4 cups dry red wine
1 1/2 cups sugar
1/4 cups Kirsch

In a medium saucepan, combine cherries, red wine, and sugar. Bring to a slow simmer over a low heat, stirring constantly. After ingredients come to a full boil, continue to cook 5 minutes. Remove from heat; let cool to room temperature.

Combine cherry-wine mixture and Kirsch in a 2-quart glass or ceramic container; cap tightly, or cover tightly with plastic wrap. Let cordial steep in a cool dark place for 1 week, swirling mixture around in container every day.

Strain cordial through sieve lined with double thickness of dampened cheesecloth into clean container. Thoroughly wash and dry original container, or have ready a second clean glass or ceramic container. Set funnel or coffee cone lined with dampened filter paper or coffee filter over container; slowly pour cordial through. When cordial is filtered to desired clarity, test for sweetness. Adjust sweetness by adding additional simple syrup. Store in an air-tight container.

WALNUT LIQUEUR

This is a delicious and inexpensive liqueur that will rival some of the commercially produced brands.

Makes about 4 cups

12 fresh walnuts
1 cinnamon stick, broken
6 whole cloves
4 cups brandy
1 cup honey

Crack open each walnut and clean out meat from the shells. Break the shells into smaller pieces. Combine walnuts, walnut shell pieces, cinnamon stick, whole cloves, a half cup of the honey, and brandy in a 2-quart glass or ceramic container. Cap tightly or cover tightly with plastic wrap. Let steep in a cool dark place 4 weeks, swirling mixture around in container every 3 days.

Strain liquid through clean sieve lined with double thickness of dampened cheesecloth into clean container. Thoroughly wash and dry original container, or have ready a second clean glass or ceramic container. Set funnel or coffee cone containing dampened filter paper or coffee filter over container; slowly pour liqueur through. Add additional half cup of honey, stirring well to combine. Cap tightly; let age 1 more month in a cool dark place.

WATERMELON LIQUEUR

A delicious reminder of summertime, this fresh and fruity liqueur can be enjoyed any time of the year.

Makes about 4 cups

**2 pounds fresh watermelon, rind removed
2 cups light rum
2 cups Simple Syrup
3 drops red food coloring (optional)
1 tablespoon glycerin**

In a large plastic or glass bowl, chop watermelon into 1-inch by 1-inch pieces, retaining as much juice as possible; remove all evidence of rind and seeds. Combine watermelon and light rum in a 2-quart glass or ceramic container; add simple syrup; stir to mix. Cap tightly, or cover tightly with plastic wrap. Let liqueur steep in a cool dark place for 4 weeks, swirling mixture around in container every other day.

Strain liqueur through sieve lined with double thickness of dampened cheesecloth into clean container. Thoroughly wash and dry original container, or have ready a second clean glass or ceramic container. Set funnel or coffee cone lined with dampened filter paper or coffee filter over container; slowly pour liqueur through. When liqueur is filtered to desired clarity, test for sweetness; add additional simple syrup to taste. Add glycerin and red food coloring, if desired; stir to mix. Cover tightly; let age an additional 2 to 4 weeks in a cool dark place.

ZUCCHINI LIQUEUR

This sounds like an unusual combination, but it has a wonderful flavor and body..

Makes about 4 cups

1 1/2 lbs. zucchini, cubed
Peel of 1 lemon, thinly sliced, pith removed
Juice of 1 lemon
1 cup water
3 cups light rum
1 cup simple syrup

In a medium saucepan, combine cubed zucchini, lemon peel, lemon juice, and water. Heat over a low flame, stirring constantly. Bring to a slow simmer, cooking until zucchini is soft, about 10 minutes. Remove from heat. Let cool.

Transfer zucchini and any remaining liquid to a large glass or ceramic container. Add rum and simple syrup; stir to mix. Cap tightly or cover tightly with plastic wrap. Age in a cool, dark place for at least 4 weeks. Shake gently each day.

Strain liquid through clean sieve lined with double thickness of dampened cheesecloth into clean container. Thoroughly wash and dry original container, or have ready a second clean glass or ceramic container. Set funnel or coffee cone containing dampened filter paper or coffee filter over container; slowly pour liqueur through. Cap tightly; let age about 1 month in a cool dark place.

Notes & My Own Recipes

Made in the USA
Las Vegas, NV
19 February 2022